The Naughty Behaviourist

Understanding Human Behaviour and How to Use It to Your Advantage

Maranda Graham

**Foreword written by Dr Ashleigh Moreland
Founder and Primary Practitioner, Re-MIND Institute**

First published by Ultimate World Publishing 2024
Copyright © 2024 Maranda Graham

ISBN

Paperback: 978-1-923255-79-1
Ebook: 978-1-923255-80-7

Maranda Graham has asserted her rights under the Copyright, Designs and Patents Act 1988 to be identified as the author of this work. The information in this book is based on the author's experiences and opinions. The publisher specifically disclaims responsibility for any adverse consequences which may result from use of the information contained herein. Permission to use information has been sought by the author. Any breaches will be rectified in further editions of the book.

All rights reserved. No part of this publication may be reproduced, stored in or introduced into a retrieval system, or transmitted in any form, or by any means (electronic, mechanical, photocopying, recording or otherwise) without the prior written permission of the author. Any person who does any unauthorised act in relation to this publication may be liable to criminal prosecution and civil claims for damages. Enquiries should be made through the publisher.

Cover design: Ultimate World Publishing
Layout and typesetting: Ultimate World Publishing
Editor: Marinda Wilkinson

Ultimate World Publishing
Diamond Creek,
Victoria Australia 3089
www.writeabook.com.au

Dedication

My beautiful mother, Jane, who loved me like no other.

My brother, Stuart, who trusted me wholeheartedly.

The two sweetest souls to grace this earth.

How blessed I have been.

Contents

Dedication	iii
Foreword	vii
Introduction	1
Chapter 1: Where Does it Come From?	3
Chapter 2: Behaviour is Communication	13
Chapter 3: The Function of Behaviour	27
Chapter 4: More About the Function of Behaviour	43
Chapter 5: Environment and Reinforcement	57
Chapter 6: Triggers	67
Chapter 7: Replacement Behaviours	79
Chapter 8: Strategies	95
Chapter 9: What About Me?	107
Chapter 10: Neurodiversity	119
Chapter 11: Summary and Pulling it all Together	129
Appendix	141
About the Author	145

Foreword

As with most of the best connections in life, I was introduced to Maranda via absolute divine intervention. Mutual friends in the coaching space recognised the alignment between our work and our shared desire to help people understand and improve human behaviour. That introduction has been a true blessing, and it is an honour to write this foreword in full support of this work getting out into the world!

What stands out to me about Maranda's approach to behaviour analysis through *The Naughty Behaviourist* is how she takes something inherently complex – often entangled with shame, trauma, guilt and hurt – and presents it in a way that honours the lived experiences of all people. She has created an accessible framework, full of practical examples and relatable scenarios, making it easy for readers to apply the concepts in their own lives.

As a neurophysiologist, therapist and coach at the Re-MIND Institute, I work with people from all walks of life, from all around the world, to process the unresolved emotions and past trauma that is driving their behaviours. While we work within a different framework, the core principle remains the same: behaviour is a form of communication. When people understand why they behave the way they do, recognising the function it serves or the need it meets, they gain the power to choose healthier, more functional responses. It's this kind of work that leads to real transformation, and through *The Naughty Behaviourist*, Maranda offers readers the tools to do just that.

This book is more than just a guide; it's honestly a gift that will keep on giving for many generations to come. For everyday people with no prior knowledge of psychology or behavioural science, Maranda has crafted a gentle, non-accusatory approach that invites readers to engage with compassion and curiosity. It will undoubtedly help improve relationships and, in turn, foster greater kindness and understanding in the world. Imagine a world where we have the emotional intelligence to respond rather than react!

What I love most about *The Naughty Behaviourist* is its simplicity. Maranda has carefully crafted her insights, real-life examples and practical tools to make this book not only easy to read but easy to implement. It provides a powerful opportunity for positive change in both individual lives and the broader community.

I encourage you to approach this book with an open mind, a readiness and strong curiosity to reflect, and a willingness to actually apply these concepts practically in your own life. Don't let this be another book that you read and do nothing with – LET it change your life. If you do, your journey ahead is one of understanding, compassion and empowerment, and I believe that, like me, you'll find yourself inspired to respond to the world around you with a heart posture of empathy and love. What could be better than that?

Dr Ashleigh Moreland
Founder and Primary Practitioner, Re-MIND Institute

Introduction

WHEN I FIRST THOUGHT OF writing a book about behaviour, I battled with who the target audience might be. I had colleagues and friends who suggested narrowing the topic to suit a particular niche, such as parenting toddlers or teenagers, intimate relationships, workplace dynamics and a plethora of other very specific cohorts. But the main idea for writing this book has always been to share my knowledge about understanding behaviour with everyday people so that they can apply it in everyday situations. I have therefore kept with my original idea and have tailored the book to just that – understanding behaviour for everyday folk.

Why write it in the first place? Well, I have always had a deep interest (almost a fascination) with people and how they work. But it's more than that. I studied a Bachelor of Social Work at university and while it paved the foundations for working with people, it didn't give me a really clear blueprint for actual behaviour. We studied multiple social work theories and approaches such as feminist theory, strengths perspective, person-centred, post-structural theory, the list goes on. But once out in the workforce, I couldn't tell you why my client was engaging in self-harm behaviours or why they were suddenly yelling at me.

The Naughty Behaviourist

It was only once I stepped into the behaviour analysis world, quite by chance, that I began to have some serious 'aha' moments. Right from the beginning I knew I was now being immersed into a powerful pool of knowledge that would change the way I viewed others, viewed myself and guided the way I work with and ultimately interact with others.

From very early in my behaviour support career, I knew that I wanted to share this knowledge so that others could use it in the same way I had. I also knew that it could easily be a very dry topic and so I set about writing the process in a way that did away with the academic jargon and the lengthy assessments. And from here *The Naughty Behaviourist* was born. The title was chosen for a few different reasons. The first one being that I wanted to steer away from the possibility of this topic being too dry. Secondly, it's a play on words, as how often have people, especially children, been labelled as 'naughty' without any real understanding of their behaviour? And the third reason is that I've never really liked being told what to do. Does anyone really? My beautiful late mother, once said to my husband with exasperation, 'Haven't you worked out by now that Maranda never does what she is told?!'. Which was quite hilarious to me. So, I've embraced that image for this book.

Reading this won't suddenly turn you into a behaviour support practitioner or an expert behaviour analyst. What it will do is provide you with a decent base understanding of what people are trying to communicate through their behaviour, how to understand it and what you can do about it. You may even be a bit like me and end up with some serious self-reflections about your own past behaviour. There's a scary thought!

Whatever you get out of it, I truly hope you enjoy it – and that you gain some insights that may just change your perspective next time you see someone behaving less than favourably.

CHAPTER 1

Where Does it Come From?

◆────────●────────◆

Have you ever stopped and looked at someone and thought, 'Why on earth are they behaving that way?'. Or thought back on a situation and wondered 'What is wrong with them?'. Or maybe you saw someone in the street acting peculiarly and muttered under your breath 'bloody idiot'. Or even, dare I say it, reflected on something you personally did and cringed?

Me too.

Human beings are creatures of an inherently social nature and daily we are faced with having to communicate with others. Unless, of course, you live as a hermit up in a wild mountain cave, only coming out to shop or trade once a month. Sounds appealing some days of the week, I'm sure, but I'm going to assume that unless this is you, you too spend a great deal of time interacting with other people on some level.

Whether you are a stay-at-home parent caring for your children, working in a busy medical ward or on a building site, studying at school or university, or travelling the world, you are interacting and communicating with others every single day. If you are anything like me, you regularly interact with people who you are completely confounded by and who behave in a manner that has you scratching (or at least shaking) your head on a regular basis. And I don't just mean strangers; I'm talking about your partners, mothers, fathers, children, workmates, bosses, clients, friends, extended family and basically any other human being you can think of.

Every single person you interact with may at some time demonstrate a behaviour that puzzles you. It might be your teenager who games all day and then slams the door in your face. Your partner who suddenly yells when having a debate about something small and simple. Your workmate who constantly gossips and talks behind people's back creating all sorts of drama. Your boss who puts you on the spot in a meeting.

But what if I could tell you the secret to what is behind the behaviour?

To teach you a set of guidelines that would have you unpacking every behaviour you come across and offering insights on how to work with it. A set of guidelines, that once understood, would allow you to have very little conflict in your life. A set of basic principles that once understood, would provide you with the tools to navigate complex situations without conflict.

Would this interest you?

It certainly interested me. I am not talking about complicated psychological theories or longwinded university journal readings. I am talking about basic principles, based on behavioural theories, and refined, to be brought to you in one easy read. One simplified book that provides you with all of this and more.

Where Does it Come From?

That's what I have for you in this book.

But let me start at the beginning. Not the beginning of time or anything as dramatic as that. But at the beginning of my journey in behaviour. And how I came to be working as a behaviourist, providing insight, assessments and outcomes for the most vulnerable of people. I'll keep it brief, so as not to bore you. I promise.

Behaviour and observing other people, has always been kind of my thing. It is born of having to navigate new social situations on a regular basis, as my parents were out of the box thinkers and we travelled and lived across Australia, New Zealand and Scotland throughout my childhood. My younger brother and I went to seven different schools in three different countries. Which is not huge in comparison to some people but was enough to tweak my initial interest in the subtle differences between these closely aligned western cultures. I mean, you would assume they would all be roughly the same.

In addition to crossing cultures, we lived across multiple different 'class' or financial contexts – sometimes living in council/government housing in almost impoverished circumstances, through to building and living in our own brand-new home. In between, we lived on the middle floor of five-star hotels my mum managed, and in a tiny motel in New Zealand, because at the time we had nowhere else to go. Adventurers at heart, my parents worked extremely hard wherever we went and I will be forever grateful for the life lessons this provided me with. While it might not seem like the most stable of home lives, my youthful adventures broadened my outlook, and my mind, and led me to an interest in human behaviour that has threaded its way into every area of my life.

In my youth, up until the age of 15, when I flew from London, England to Adelaide, Australia alone, I spent time amongst a rather broad range of people. This included people with a disability (physical, mental and psychosocial) living in the community and being accepted and protected (and sometimes ridiculed) by the people around them, all the way through to people who were deemed to be 'old money', who owned land and properties. I even had family who were self-professed 'poachers' of the land (in fact one of my uncles once wrote a book called *Poacher's Pie*, regaling his adventures on the land). I also had family who worked regular jobs, tirelessly, in order to own and maintain their homes and lifestyle.

Every interaction and experience I had along the way further developed my interest in human behaviour and guided me toward my work in this space.

In 1991, I arrived in Tasmania at the age of 15, completed some schooling, married a local boy and promptly had five children. I then turned my mind to gaining a university education. Initially, I looked at a straight psychology degree but after digging deeper into my own likes and interests I went with a Bachelor of Social Work. I graduated from university and spent a few years working in homelessness, including a year working 12-hour overnight shifts in a crisis accommodation shelter, for young men aged 13–18. As the sole worker responsible overnight for up to six young men, I learnt fast and further developed my keen interest in behaviour. This job was not for the faint-hearted and it remains one of my favourite jobs of my career. It was so much fun!

After many years of observing and working with human beings, I thought I had a decent understanding of what drove people to behave the way they do and how to support those being impacted by the behaviour of others. It wasn't until I fell (or was divinely guided) into behaviour support that I had a light-bulb moment and stumbled across a formula that can be applied to almost anyone and almost any situation. Behaviour support suddenly pulled everything together for me. I simply can't wait to take you through this book to teach you that you do not need to have a university education to understand the key principles of behaviour analysis – and you certainly do not need to study it for hours or use a multitude of assessments in order to gain your own insight into why someone is behaving the way they are and understand what you can do about it.

Before I launch into the first key component, which is communication, I think it's important that we touch on where it all comes from.

In Australia, the National Disability Insurance Scheme (NDIS), which is jointly governed by both state and federal governments, provide varied supports through funding packages. The support that I provide is 'behaviour support' and I am known as a behaviour support practitioner. There are thousands of behaviour support practitioners working around Australia to provide functional behaviour analysis to people with a disability who have what is known as 'behaviours of concern'. We also monitor and assess any restrictive practice being utilised to support a person with a disability to ensure that it is ethical and reasonable. Our goal is always to fade out the restriction, such as having access to knives or other sharp implements, through analysing the behaviours and providing strategies and alternative ways to have their needs met. It's a really interesting job that is very complex and includes assessments and criteria that ensure ethical practice.

Behaviour support was developed in Australia based on behavioural analysis, sometimes known as applied behaviour analysis (ABA). Certainly, the main principles of ABA have been greatly utilised in the actual functional assessments. However, as practitioners we branch far further out from ABA and incorporate a truly person-centred approach to all the work that we do. This is important, as in recent years there has been a lot of push back and some pretty ugly media focus on circumstances where a pure ABA approach has been misused creating some awful circumstances for very vulnerable people. It's therefore essential to look at every situation broadly and see how we can support a person's human rights first and foremost.

To give you a further overview of this whole journey, I'm going to skip a few steps in the progression of behaviour analysis (plus a few centuries) to briefly touch on the development of behaviour analysis. I don't want to get too academic so I will only provide a brief overview. If you are really interested in reading about this further, I recommend searching each theorist's name and what they were known for.

Without being disrespectful by excluding other theorists who have come in between, there are four significant historical men who through their extensive research contributed to the way we view and assess behaviour today. A word of warning though, many of the experiments were conducted in a time where there were no ethics committees to answer to!

The first mention is to Ivan Pavlov (26 September 1849 – 27 February 1936), a Russian and Soviet experimental neurologist and physiologist. He completed experiments involving dogs and you will hear the term 'Pavlov's dogs' in reference. Basically, Pavlov was known primarily for his work in what is known as 'classical conditioning'. Classical conditioning is the process where an automatic response occurs in relation to a specific stimulus. For example, when you take your dog for a walk you may use a leash. As time goes on your dog becomes conditioned to know that when you pick up that leash (or dare say the word 'walk') that means they are going for a walk. For more information, search Pavlov's dogs and even explore your local library as there are many books out there on this topic.

The second mention goes to Edward Thorndike (31 August 1874 – 9 August 1949), an American psychologist who was most famously known for his puzzle box experiments on cats. Thorndike became known for his theory of 'law and effect' and what is really interesting about Thorndike is that his experiments provided us with evidence that a positive reinforcer for behaviour is much stronger than a negative reinforcer. Basically, this means that someone praised or rewarded for their behaviour is more likely to repeat the behaviour

Where Does it Come From?

than someone who has been punished for it. I think of Thorndike and chuckle when I watch the episode of the sitcom, *The Big Bang Theory*, where Sheldon is conditioning his free-spirited neighbour, Penny, by providing her with treats every time she has a behaviour that Sheldon approves of. It all goes well until Leonard, Penny's love interest, cottons on to what is happening.

The third mention goes to John Watson (9 January 1878 – 25 September 1958), another American psychologist who contributed significantly to the behaviour analysis world and gets credit for the development of the psychological school of behaviourism. What is notable is that Watson was highly interested in the environment within which a behaviour occurs, which is something I talk about later in this book. Watson, however, is also famous for a very dubious but effective experiment known as the 'Little Albert' experiment. Through this experiment Watson was able to demonstrate that classical conditioning was possible in humans as well as animals. If you need a good late-night cry, have a search and read up on the Little Albert experiment. Certainly not the most unethical experiment out there but definitely one that contributes to our need for strong ethical oversight.

The fourth and final mention goes to B.F. Skinner (20 March 1904 – 18 August 1990), known as the 'father' of behaviour analysis. Skinner was an American psychologist, behaviourist and social philosopher. Skinner is well known for his 'Skinner Box' experiment, which is not as scary as it sounds. Skinner used a wooden box and hungry rats to develop his theory of 'operant conditioning', which essentially suggests that behaviour and learning can be changed using reward and punishment. He was really focused on the premise that classical conditioning could not be the only way to explain the complexity of human behaviour. He also focused on the environment and how this impacts human behaviour.

Why am I telling you about these men? I am giving you this information so that you can really understand that what I am about to teach you is not just mumbo jumbo that I made up whilst sipping a gin on a random Saturday night. It is based on sound theoretical knowledge that is still relevant to today's understanding of human behaviour. It forms the basis of what we know and use as behaviourists, albeit with a more ethical and person-centred lens applied.

This is about as academic and techy as I want to get in this book. I promised you an easy-to-understand set of tools and that's what I'm going to give you. But before I jump into it, I just wanted to touch on a couple of features I have added to make this journey a little easier. The first one is a chapter overview with the key points so you can jump back at any time and remind yourself of what I talked about. This is at the end of each chapter under the heading 'toolbox takeaways'. The second thing I want to point out is that this book is in layers. A little bit like Shrek's onion but we are not peeling the layers off, we are adding layers. So, for this book I am going to use a toolbox metaphor. The toolbox works for me because I have a husband and two sons who are automotive mechanics and a father who is a builder, so my brain likes this. To understand the fullness of what I am saying you are going to need the full toolbox. Without the full toolbox and the range of tools we are adding you will not be able to 'do the job', or you will be limited in doing the job. This chapter so far forms the 'toolbox', but it's empty right now. By the time you reach the end of Chapter 11, your toolbox will be full and you will be well on your way to changing how you see others and their behaviours.

So, let's begin.

Where Does it Come From?

Toolbox takeaways

- This chapter's background information provides you with the empty toolbox that is the foundation of where behaviour analysis and my role in it has come from.
- Curiosity about behaviour is where it all begins.
- The foundational ideas by psychological theorists are still relevant to today's understanding of behaviour.
- Classical conditioning, operant conditioning and law and effect are key terms in psychological behaviour analysis.
- Behaviours of concern is a term used by the National Disability Insurance Scheme (NDIS) to describe any behaviours that are deemed 'undesirable behaviours'.
- Applied Behaviour Analysis (ABA), which forms a lot of the foundations of understanding behaviour, it is not as popular as it once was in providing alternatives to behaviour.

CHAPTER 2

Behaviour is Communication

---◆—————●—————◆---

THE VERY FIRST THING I want you to understand that is imperative to understanding behaviour, is that **every behaviour is a form of communication**. Stay with me on this, I promise it's true.

Communication comes in many forms. There are four main types of communication: verbal, non-verbal, visual and written communication. Behaviour can sit within all four types. For example, being verbally aggressive: yelling, swearing, screaming, would sit under verbal communication. Whereas someone yawning might sit under non-verbal communication. Writing someone a threatening letter could sit under written communication. Do you see what I mean?

When we observe a behaviour in someone, it's important to know that they are actually trying to communicate something. They may be doing this consciously or unconsciously but the key thing is to know they are communicating *something*. For some people it may be that they are communicating their needs, for others their frustrations and for some their emotions. One thing we do know is that some things are much harder than others to communicate through simply talking. Sometimes when someone is yelling or screaming or generally being aggressive in nature, they are trying to tell us something that is hard to communicate in words.

For people who have a disability or are neurodivergent, they may use their behaviour a lot more than people who are neurotypical to communicate their needs. This is for a number of reasons that I'll touch on in Chapter 10. Our job is to understand that behaviour equals communication and to attempt to understand what is being communicated. Additionally, people who are intoxicated or under the influence of other substances will often use their behaviour as communication more than those who are fully sober. This can be due to the substance inhibiting their expressive and/or their receptive language.

- Expressive language = what you speak out to others
- Receptive language = what you understand as language coming back to you

They, therefore, are unable to fully articulate what they want to say using language. Those under the influence of substances can also have challenges with regulating their emotions in the usual manner, which further increases their communication by behaviour as opposed to using verbal language. How often do you see fights break out in pubs or outside pubs when people have been drinking heavily. Often over things that could have been communicated easily with words had they been sober.

> Behaviour = Communication

Behaviour is Communication

Let's look at some examples of how behaviour is communicating something. Then I will give you some tips on how to work out what is being communicated.

Example 1

Jasper is sitting in a meeting with his lawyer. Things are becoming increasingly negative and suddenly Jasper leaps up, picks up his drink bottle, throws it at a wall and storms out of the room.

What is Jasper communicating?

I'd assume that he's trying to communicate his extreme anger and frustration and perhaps has reached a point where he can no longer regulate his emotions. Simple right?

Let's try another one.

Example 2

A toddler, let's call them Taylor, is in the highchair and has been eating some food from a bowl. Taylor is struggling to reach the last bit of food using the spoon. Suddenly, they up end the bowl to the floor and start crying.

What is Taylor trying to communicate?

I'm thinking that Taylor is trying to communicate their frustration at not being able to use the spoon as well as they'd like and probably doesn't have the expressive language skills to verbalise this.

Let's try one a little more complicated.

Example 3

Sam, a teenage girl, arrives at school and her friends tell her that they all have a maths test in third period. Sam has forgotten about the test and has not studied at all. Maths is not her favourite subject and she starts to feel upset, possibly anxious about attending class, taking the test and ultimately failing. Sam tries to text her mum, as she often does, to help her manage this but she realises she is out of phone credit and the message does not go through. Sam decides to skip the class and spends the entire period in the toilets. She ends up with a detention when she is caught out.

What is Sam trying to communicate?

Sam is trying to communicate that she is scared about attending class, scared of failing and possibly needs some more time.

I'd like to point out here that often behaviour is the part you see. It is the result of not being able to communicate through talking or writing or gesturing. Someone might jump up and down excitedly because they are overwhelmed with emotion and don't know the words to express their delight. Another person might cry because they are needing to communicate that they are sad but don't have the words to express it.

Behaviour as a form of communication is like an iceberg. What you see above the water is the behaviour. Under the water is what the person is trying to communicate.

Behaviour is Communication

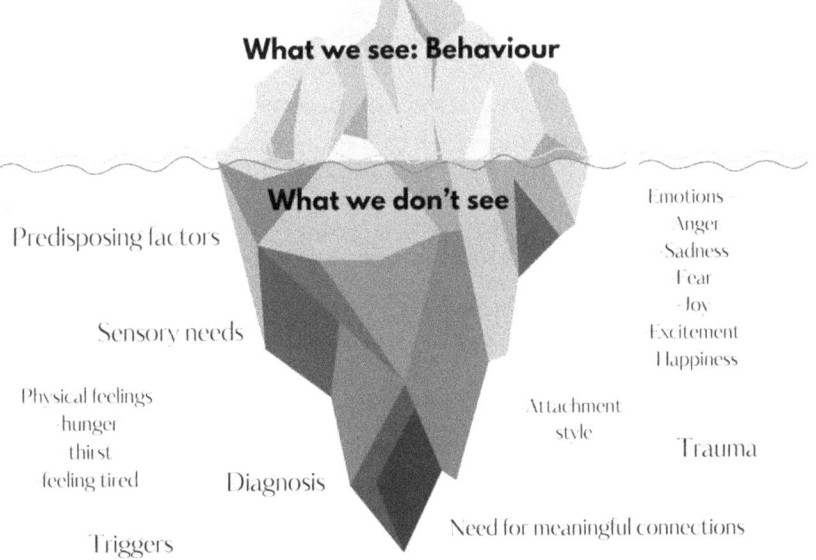

This is not to say that people can't become really great communicators. They certainly can. It's more about understanding that in addition to talking, writing, body language and non-verbal communication, behaviour should also be understood as a means of communication. So often we just punish people (especially children and youth) for demonstrating undesirable behaviours. In adults, we ignore them, talk about them, judge them, walk away from them and sometimes punish them. Don't get me wrong, I am not saying that behaviours that are illegal or a crime should not be punished or have some type of consequence, just that we can understand that by responding to a behaviour and considering what is being communicated, we may never get to the point of having to provide a consequence or feel uncomfortable around the person.

What if we used *understanding* the behaviours of people to find out what they are really trying to communicate instead of ignoring them, talking about them or walking away from them? That could really change the outcomes of some of our interactions. Once you are aware that through their behaviour, someone is attempting to communicate something, it really changes the way that you view behaviour. This is true for children and adults. It enhances relationships because you are reframing a behaviour instead of reacting to it. I recommend that you practise this over the course of reading this book and start thinking about what that person might be communicating.

Let's take a look at some more examples, to see how this can work for relationships.

Example 4

You arrive at your sister's home and she seems not like her usual self. She seems really flat. She makes you a coffee but slumps down in her chair, shoving the washing basket out of the way with her leg as she does so and sits with her head in her hand and her elbow propped up on the arm of the chair. As she does this, she sighs deeply and says, 'I just can't handle anything at the moment'.

What do you think she is trying to communicate?

I'd be wondering if she is trying to communicate her exhaustion, overwhelm or stress. And that maybe she needs some support or a break. She's certainly not communicating that she is excited about something.

And before we go any further, I just want to caution you at this stage about making assumptions. Be very careful when considering what someone is trying to communicate, in case you get it wrong and cause further upset. If In doubt, ask. People will usually tell you if you've gotten it wrong.

Example 5

You attend the cemetery to visit a loved one's grave. As you arrive you see an elderly gentleman sitting on a park bench under a tree. You can see that his shoulders are slumped forward, his head is hanging low and he has tears in his eyes. He is peeling petals off an old bunch of flowers and letting them fall slowly to the ground.

Now I know with this one you may be thinking 'that's his body language, not behaviour' and you would be partly correct. Yes, it is his body language, but as discussed earlier, body language is also behaviour.

So, what is this man trying to communicate?

My best guess would be that he is trying to communicate that he is sad, perhaps lonely. He may also be communicating that he wants to be left alone, or he may be communicating that he would like some company. If I felt safe to do so, I might spark a short conversation to see if he communicates a little bit more through language so I'd know if he's trying to be alone or if he is seeking company.

This one is an example of indirect communication. The man is not actually deliberately trying to communicate with you but he is communicating through his behaviour, nonetheless.

Example 6

Children are really good communicators, not always through language, and not always in rational ways in our adult minds. I thoroughly enjoy random TikToks and videos that say 'reasons my toddler is upset' with a range of completely irrational reasons for us to chuckle over. But rational or not, children are communicating something to us.

You have taken your 4-year-old to the park for a play. It is time to leave and go home for lunch and a nap. You open the car door and they suddenly go rigid. Rigid as a board and you are unable to get them to sit in their car seat. It may be combined with some crying or even some thrashing.

What is your child trying to communicate?

Pretty simple really. They are trying to communicate that they do not want to leave, they were likely having fun and they don't know when they can come back again. There are some good strategies to help with all of these situations but I want to keep that until late in the book so not to confuse the process.

Let's talk about *really* bad behaviour

If all behaviour is communication, I hear you ask, then what about really bad behaviour? Well, for the purpose of analysing behaviour, this does include all behaviour. In fact, the beautiful thing about behaviour analysis is that it works for almost any person, any situation, any behaviour.

However, I want to make this clear. Just because we can analyse the behaviour and work out what someone is trying to communicate, it doesn't mean it's right, it doesn't mean it's legal and it doesn't necessarily give justification to the behaviour. Right at this point we are merely trying to work out what the person is trying to communicate through their behaviour.

I think it's important that we do go over some behaviours that are at the pointier end so you can see that the process still applies. Again, this does not justify them in any way. But it is important to demonstrate how to look at a behaviour without judgement to purely see what is being communicated. Tricky, I know.

I'd like to offer a trigger warning here – discussion of physically aggressive and violent behaviour. If this is a trigger for you then you may like to skip this next example.

Example 7

You have gone out for a meal and drinks with some friends. There are a table of six people over in the corner and they are having a debate about politics. I choose politics because honestly no-one can agree on this and we all have differing opinions. One person in particular is becoming increasingly argumentative and loud, he is upset about the latest tax changes as this is going to significantly increase his tax bill and lead to some serious money issues for his family.

His friend is arguing that the tax increases are needed and it's important that the higher income earners are taxed at a higher rate.

The argument ends with one person storming out of the restaurant with the other one following him, some pushing and shoving occurs and the first man ends up punching his friend in the jaw and knocking him to the ground.

Not the best way to behave, I know, but let's stick with it as this type of situation is unfortunately quite common.

What is the first man trying to communicate?

Your initial response might be to say, 'He's trying to communicate that he's an idiot' or that 'he's trying to communicate that he can't control himself'. But I think we should dig a little deeper.

I think he's trying to communicate that he is scared. I think he is trying to communicate that he feels out of control and I think he is trying to communicate that he's possibly hurt that his friend would think something is okay that could potentially ruin him.

You see how our first responses are loaded with judgement, which is, honestly, quite understandable. But if we can take away the initial judgement of what has happened, we can view the behaviour as a form of communication. And from there, once we can identify what a person is communicating, we can make changes so that this especially bad behaviour can be reduced or eliminated in the future.

I could provide a hundred examples of really undesirable behaviour but I don't want to sensationalise it. Instead, I'd like you to start thinking about incidents where you have either witnessed or been part of a behaviour that is really undesirable. See if you can think about what the person might have been communicating, either consciously or unconsciously.

It's all communication – good or bad

At this point, I'd like to expand on the idea of behaviour as communication to include *positive* behaviour. So far, we have only looked at undesirable behaviours and I think it's important that we look at more desirable behaviours, 'good' behaviours and behaviours we'd like to see more of. We tend to focus on the undesirable behaviours as most of the time we would really like them to cease, or at least change. Undesirable behaviours are more obvious to us because they often prompt a reaction in us of shock, surprise, frustration or anger. Positive or more desirable behaviours keep us feeling good and so are not noticed as often as undesirable behaviours. Make sense?

Let's unpack a few examples of more desirable behaviours to see if the idea of 'behaviour is communication' is true.

Example 8

Sally's mother has just passed away. She is sitting at home and not feeling great. She is trying to plan the funeral and it's hard.

Behaviour is Communication

Her friend arrives with a bunch of flowers and something for dinner that evening.

What is her friend trying to communicate?

My guess is that she is trying to communicate that she cares about her friend and wants to make things easier in the only way she knows how.

Another friend arrives, she doesn't bring flowers or food or a card. But she offers to take Sally's children to the park for a play. She takes the two small children to the park for a few hours and returns them, showers them, feeds them dinner and helps to put them to bed.

What is this friend trying to communicate?

The same thing as the first friend would be my assessment. Just in a different way.

Example 9

You are working in a classroom of youth with a particularly rowdy group and you are struggling to engage the class. One of the youths move to a spare seat at the front of the class and attempts to focus on what you are saying. They regularly turn around to shoosh the others. Throughout the lesson they raise their hand and answer questions as well as asking for clarification. At the end of the lesson, as they leave, they say 'thanks Mr Smith'.

What is the youth communicating?

I would be thinking that they are trying to communicate that they are enjoying your lesson, that they understand your frustrations and that they want to help you by being attentive.

Positive or more desirable behaviour is often easier to analyse and it's worth touching on as once you understand what is being communicated, such as caring and kindness, this can really enhance your experience of life too. It can be challenging to initially understand what someone is trying to communicate and so I've added this table to give you some initial suggestions.

Behaviour	What is being communicated?
Verbal aggression – yelling, swearing, shouting, threats	Possibilities include: - Fear - Anger - Frustration
Physical Aggression – hitting, punching, kicking, throwing things	Often associated with - Fear - Anger - Feeling out of control

Once we understand behaviour as communication, we have added our first tool to our toolbox. We can then add then another layer, the function of the behaviour, in the next chapter. So, grab a drink, settle in and see what you make of it.

Behaviour is Communication

Toolbox takeaways

- All behaviour is communicating something.
- Behaviour can communicate in positive or negative ways.
- Behaviour communication is like an iceberg, the behaviour can be seen above the water and what is being communicated sits below the water.
- Just because a behaviour is illegal or morally abhorrent, doesn't mean we can't work out what is being communicated.
- Communication through behaviour can be conscious or unconscious.
- People under the influence of substances will communicate with their behaviour more than those who are sober.

Behaviour Toolbox

What is the person communicating through their behaviour?

CHAPTER 3

The Function of Behaviour

THE FUNCTION OF A BEHAVIOUR. What is that? The function of behaviour is possibly the most important tool you will be adding to your toolbox. It can be a little tricky to understand but it will make sense as I go along.

The function of behaviour is a category that the behaviour can be *understood within*. The function of a behaviour is essentially the WHY of the behaviour. There is some debate within the behaviour world about how many functions there are; some argue four, some five and some even argue six functions. For the purpose of this book, I will be using five functions of behaviour. Mainly because it's what I am used to and they make sense in my head.

The five functions of behaviour are:

Attention (Attention needing, connection seeking, interaction)

Tangible (Access to things, like people, places, outcomes)

Escape (Avoiding things, like people, places, outcomes, tasks)

Non-social (Sensory, automatic, habitual)

Physical (In response to physical challenges such as pain attenuation, illness, hunger)

Any behaviour that you can observe or be around will fall into one or more of these categories. These are a little challenging to understand to begin with, and one of the things I want to do in this book is to reframe what we are going to call them. There's a couple of reasons for doing this, which I will explain.

I like to change the name of 'attention', mainly because it carries a negative connotation with 'attention seeking'. Attention seeking is seen as a negative behaviour and we've all heard it used in this way. I like to reframe it as 'interaction' as that is essentially what the person is trying to communicate. That they require an interaction with you, or whoever else is there. Interaction is just a much nicer way of outlining what the person is asking for with their behaviour. Just keep the idea of attention at the back of your mind for this one though, as sometimes it's a better descriptor of what is happening.

'Tangible' is being renamed as 'access', which is an easier term to understand. It's really describing exactly what the person is trying to communicate, which is access to something – a person, an item, a place. By using access, it describes it better than tangible as people often use the word tangible in their everyday lives to describe something physical or something that can be seen. So, to avoid confusion, I will use access for this.

The Function of Behaviour

'Non-social' will be reframed as 'automatic' as it makes much more sense than a weirdly described non-social. Using the term non-social means that it is the most challenging one to understand but by reframing it, it becomes much easier.

'Physical' will remain the same as it's pretty self-explanatory and 'escape' will just be used interchangeably with avoidance as they are both easy to understand but sometimes one suits the situation a bit better.

Let's take a look at our five functions now that they have been reframed.

Function	What is covers	Also known as
Interaction	Attention needing, connection seeking, interaction needing/seeking	*Attention*
Access	Access to desired people, things, locations, outcomes	*Tangible*
Escape	Avoiding certain people, locations, tasks, outcomes	*Escape*
Automatic	Sensory need, automatic, habitual	*Non-social*
Physical	Pain attenuation, injury, illness, hunger	*Physical*

You might be wondering why I have bothered to give you the original descriptions that are used in behaviour analysis. Why not just teach you the adapted ones I have listed? The reason is that I want you to be able to take your knowledge and use it interchangeably if you are to pick up some other formal behaviour analysis document or book. Understanding that they are sometimes used interchangeably is important for all future reading.

Now that I have given you the five functions, let's unpack each of them a bit more.

Interaction/attention

Interaction or attention needing is all about gaining the level of attention that is needed at the time. It is about having an interaction with another person, someone who the person is desiring to have an interaction with. In my work as a behaviour support practitioner, I often talk about this one being about connection seeking. This is especially true in the disability sector as many people with a disability live in relative isolation and what I mean by that is that many of their everyday interactions are with a range of support people, such as support workers, physiotherapists, speech pathologists or therapists, psychologists, psychiatrists, general practitioners, occupational therapists and social workers. My goal is therefore to remind those working directly with someone with a disability to ensure that they are providing the person with a deeper interaction. Make sense?

For people who are able bodied and neurotypical, the idea remains the same. As I discussed at the beginning of Chapter 1, human beings are social creatures. Our society has evolved rapidly in the last 10 to 20 years to become unbelievably virtual-based. It is quite astonishing how quickly this occurred. I would love to study human behaviour in another 10 years to see the differences in the way people interact compared with that of the 1990s even. One area that concerns me is loneliness, or isolation. I studied loneliness at university and it was heartbreaking. With so many things now being accessible online, I can't imagine how much more this has impacted people who were already isolated.

But I digress.

What people are seeking is connection. They can achieve this through relationships and everyday interactions. For some people a very small amount of interaction or connection is enough, for others it can be a deeper need. But whatever level of connection they need, some people will seek this through their behaviours, either consciously or unconsciously.

Let's go through some examples of interaction/attention being the function.

Example 1

You are attempting to cook dinner and your small child, let's say age 4, is standing right next to your leg, whining, then crying and then eventually falls to the floor thrashing and sobbing.

Now we are going to start using some steps with our tools so we get in the habit of it.

Step 1: Ask yourself 'What are they trying to communicate?'

> Answer: Probably that they are tired and that they need you. But they are also communicating the function.

Step 2: Consider what the function is. In this instance the *function* of the behaviour is **interaction/attention**.

I will be adding the other steps as we go along so that you can see what we can do about it and how we can work it to your advantage or reduce the behaviour.

In this situation, the child is communicating that they are needing your connection/interaction/attention. Why are they not just saying this? Probably because being so tired, they are not as regulated as they usually are and so usual processes go out the window.

Example 2

You have a work friend who when you are having a conversation with them about a report you are writing, continuously turns the conversation around to what they are writing and eventually starts to talk to you about their personal life.

Step 1: What are they trying to communicate?

> Answer: It's not as easy to work out with this one but my best guess would be that they are trying to communicate that they need someone to talk to, or maybe that they are feeling alone. Or even that they actually like your company. As adults we are often guilty of assuming that people do not like us when it's often the opposite.

Step 2: Consider what the function is. In this example, the function is **interaction/attention.** They seem to be seeking a connection with you OR just seeking someone who will hear what they have to say. Either way, the function is **interaction/attention.**

Example 3

I want to touch on this example because it's something I get asked about a lot and it's something that has happened to a LOT of people.

You discover that some people you know have been talking about you behind your back. It was nasty gossipy stuff and in fact they have even added some more false information to the story they were discussing about you. You are understandably upset by it. But the process of analysing it can actually help.

Step 1: What were they trying to communicate?

>Answer: They were trying to communicate that they know something about you that no-one else does, therefore they feel socially superior in that moment with whoever they are sharing the information with.

Step 2: Consider what the function is. In this example the function of the behaviour is **interaction/attention**. This may seem like a stretch but consider that by talking about you behind your back they are actually seeking to make a deeper connection with those they are talking with. It gives them a sense of social superiority and actually enhances their connection and acceptance in the group or relationship. Most gossip is about connection with others at the disadvantage of someone. A bit sad but it happens.

TIP: The best way I can explain the function of interaction/attention is to describe it as: someone attempting to gain a level of attention or an interaction to meet their needs, whatever that need is.

Access/tangible

The function of access or tangible is one of the easiest to understand and apply. However, there are some outliers that can be a bit tricky. Especially when we get into behaviours that have more than one function, which I will go into in more detail in the next chapter.

Access is all about someone trying to communicate that they are needing/wanting access to a particular person, like their mum or a friend; needing/wanting access to a particular location, like a concert, the park, a shop; needing/wanting access to an item such as their phone, food, drink, a toy and needing/wanting access to an outcome such as being given permission to do something, a promotion, not having to leave the park (think of our child example in Chapter 2).

Let's go through some examples of access/tangible being the function of the behaviour.

Example 1

You are in line at the store and someone cuts in front of you. You say politely, 'excuse me, I was in line first'. They ignore you and stay in the queue and are served before you and then go on their way.

Step 1: What are they trying to communicate?

> Answer: Whether justified or not they are communicating that their needs are greater than yours (in their opinion) at that point in time. Perhaps they are also communicating that they are in a hurry. Remember what I said earlier about behaviours sometimes being illegal or 'bad'. In this case they are behaving outside the social moral code, which is technically unwritten and so can be breached any time anyone wants to.

Step 2: Consider what the function is. In this case the function is **access/tangible** as they are trying to gain access to a better outcome than they had before, which is being served faster. Unfortunately, you were the fall guy, but when we are working out the communication and the function, we have to try to take out the emotion of it, even if it's just momentarily.

Example 2

Let's do a simple one. You are in the supermarket and your preteen daughter has asked for a voucher for a gaming pass for her Xbox. You tell her that she cannot have this and continue to go around the shop. She goes very quiet and doesn't speak. When you ask her what is wrong, she says 'nothing'. After a while she asks you again if she can have this. Again, you say no. She remains quiet and doesn't speak for the rest of the outing.

Step 1: What is she trying to communicate?

>Answer: She is trying to communicate that she is very unhappy with your decision to say no to her request.

Step 2: Consider what the function is. The function of the behaviour (the quiet sulking/resistance) is **access/tangible**. The reason it is **access/tangible** is she is using the behaviour to try to communicate that she would like access to the gaming pass. Final point on this one – consider what would happen if you eventually bought the gaming pass after she had demonstrated the behaviour? You'd be reinforcing this behaviour as an effective way of getting access to something she wants. I'll talk about reinforcement in later chapters but something to consider for now.

Escape/avoidance

The function of escape/avoidance is just as easy to determine as access/tangible. Escape is all about a person attempting to communicate their avoidance of a particular person, like a teacher, someone they have previously upset, or someone who makes them feel uncomfortable; avoiding a particular location such as the dentist, or somewhere they feel unsafe; avoiding a task such as a report that is due, paying a phone bill, doing a chore; avoiding an outcome such as avoiding finishing a car restoration, avoiding opening exam results. A hint here is – procrastination has an **escape/avoidance** function. And why do we do it? It's an effective tool to meet our needs. Why wouldn't we?

Let's touch on a couple of examples for the escape function.

Example 1

An argument has occurred between yourself and your partner. It is happening because you want to have an explanation for why a large amount of money has been spent from your accounts without discussion (let's say you have an agreement that you consult with each other on anything more than $1000 spend). But in this instance, they did not consult with you and bought an item. The argument is becoming heated. They start yelling and swearing at you and eventually they walk out, slam the door HARD and drive off in their car, returning hours later.

Step 1: What are they trying to communicate?

> Answer: They are trying to communicate that they don't want to have to talk about this. They are possibly trying to communicate that they don't have an explanation for their behaviour and they are possibly trying to communicate through their behaviour that they feel annoyed that you are questioning them so intently on this.

Step 2: What is the function of their behaviour? The function is clearly **escape/avoidance**. They want to escape the conversation and avoid the conflict. Simple right?

Example 2

Your children are fighting, yelling and arguing about whose turn it is to sit in the front of the car (obviously they are all old enough to legally sit in the front for this example). You are tired of this and step in. You lay out a sudden genius rule that from now on, whoever is the oldest person with you, gets to sit in the front.

Step 1: What are you trying to communicate?

Answer: You are trying to communicate to your children that you have had enough of this argument time after time.

Step 2: What is the function of your behaviour? It's **escape.** You are trying to communicate your need to escape the noise and the arguing. Oh, and the function of your children's behaviour? Can you guess? Yep, it's **access/tangible.** They are each attempting to communicate their need/want to be in the front of the car and thereby demonstrate to their siblings that they have won and they are superior. Well, that's what I would have been thinking as a child. How about you?

Automatic/non-social

Automatic function is all about meeting a need within you. Automatic function is about something from within that is driving the behaviour, whereas interaction/attention, access/tangible and escape/avoidance are all based on responding to the environment. Automatic function as well as physical function, to a degree, occur regardless of the environment. Let me explain this one a bit further.

Let's say you are at the bank and you have been waiting at the counter for an extended period while the teller goes to find out some additional information for you. You find yourself becoming impatient and realise that you have been tapping your fingernails rapidly on the counter. This is an automatic behaviour. Or you have been out all day, first at work and then had to do some Christmas shopping in a busy and crowded mall, followed by driving home through peak hour traffic. As soon as you get home you curl up on the couch with a huge blanket on you. This is an automatic behaviour as it is driven from somewhere inside you that is seeking the relief of quiet and possibly some pressure on you – they are self-regulatory behaviours. Automatic function of behaviour is internally reinforced so can often be the hardest to change, however not impossible. Understanding the behaviour is key to changing it.

Let's take a look at a couple of examples for the automatic function.

Example 1

You have an exam and you are standing outside the exam hall waiting to be let in. You notice that your friend is looking rather pale and you see that they have started to crack their knuckles over and over while pacing back and forth.

Step 1: What are they communicating through their behaviour?

>Answer: They are likely communicating that they are nervous or anxious about the exam.

Step 2: What is the function of the behaviour? It is **automatic**. They are using this behaviour automatically as it is an effective tool to meet their needs. And what are their needs in this moment? To reduce their anxiety or nervousness by a self-soothing technique that they have likely used many times before. Would this work for everyone? Absolutely not but that doesn't matter as long as it works for them.

Example 2

You arrive on the scene of a two-car crash. Everyone is okay. You notice that a female driver of one of the cars is sitting off to the side of the road on the ground and you notice that she has her arms around herself and is gently rocking backwards and forwards.

Step 1: What is she communicating through her behaviour?

>Answer: She is communicating her distress and her need for comfort.

Step 2: What is the function of the behaviour? It is **automatic**. She is using this behaviour automatically to help to regulate herself in a self-soothing manner. She may have never used this behaviour before but it obviously feels like the right thing to do to meet her need of feeling more regulated and most likely managing her complex emotions in the moment.

Are you starting to see the process becoming easier as we go through the examples? Simple right? It is when you break it all down step by step. Let's jump briefly into the final function of physical and then we will dig a bit deeper in the next chapter where I'll provide examples of behaviours that have more than one function and what to do when you are not sure which one is the most important.

Physical

Not every behaviour analysist assesses for *physical* as one of the functions. The reason for this is that when you are completing a full functional behaviour assessment, you look at every aspect of the environment, the physiology and the health/mental health including diagnosis. So, any physical issues such as pain is taken care of. For the purpose of this book and my goal for this book being to bring behaviour analysis to you in a simplified version, we are not able to complete a full functional behaviour assessment – that would be a whole other, much longer book. I feel it is worth adding physical here as a function so that you can more easily analyse the person's behaviour and understand it.

The function of physical is fairly easy to understand and like the function of automatic, it is internally reinforced. That means that it can occur regardless of the environment the person is in. It can be as simple as a person having a headache and then yelling at someone because their head hurts. But let's run over the examples to make sure we are on the same page.

The Naughty Behaviourist

Example 1

Your teenager arrives home from school. They are grumpy and have not spoken much so far. You ask them how their day went and they snap at you and chuck their bag down on the kitchen floor with gusto. Now for the purpose of this example we are going to assume that there is nothing else happening at school such as bullying.

Step 1: What are they trying to communicate though their behaviour?

> Answer: They are likely communicating that they are not feeling great and that they need to eat.

Step 2: What is the function of the behaviour? The function of the behaviour is **physical**. They are feeling physically affected by not eating and by being hungry.

I experienced a classic example of this one when one of my sons arrived home from his grade seven school camp. I picked him up from school, on a Friday afternoon, after an intensive week of hiking and rock climbing, along with his very heavy pack and we headed off. I began to get worried as I drove along as my usually very talkative son was very, very quiet. He also looked extremely out of sorts and honestly my mind started to turn to all of the horrendous things that could have possibly happened to him whilst under the care of his school for an entire week. To the point that I started to question him about his safety and experiences on camp. Needless to say, all was well. I took him via the local fast-food drive through where he guzzled copious amounts of unhealthy, high-energy food and drink. He then slept for about 14 hours straight and was right as rain when he finally woke up. The function of his unusual behaviour was definitely **physical**.

Example 2

You arrive at work on Monday morning and there's a vibe happening. The rest of your team indicates that the boss is on the warpath today. You avoid contact with them until you have no choice. You head into their office and discuss a situation about your client. It ends in your boss snapping at you and you exit the office. You later find out that your boss sprained their ankle over the weekend and this is reinforced when you see that they are actually hobbling along the hallway with a crutch under one arm.

Step 1: What are they communicating through their behaviour?

> Answer: They are communicating that they are in pain and their tolerance is likely lower than usual.

Step 2: What is the function of the behaviour? It is **physical**. They are behaving in that manner due to a physical sensation in their body. As we discussed earlier, we are taking all emotion out of this analysis for the sake of the process. It doesn't mean we have to agree with the behaviour in order to analyse it.

In the next chapter, I am going to expand on the functions of behaviour by providing you with examples of behaviour that have more than one function. But for now, let's have a look at this chapter's takeaways.

Toolbox takeaways

- Steps to analysing a person's behaviour are:
  - Step 1: What are they trying to communicate through their behaviour?
  - Step 2: What is the function of the behaviour?
- There are five functions of behaviour – interaction/attention, access/tangible, escape/avoidance, automatic/sensory and physical.
- Understanding the function enables us to work out the WHY of the behaviour.
- Knowing the function can help us know how to respond to a behaviour to either eliminate it or reduce it.
- Understanding the behaviour and knowing the function doesn't mean we have to agree with it or the person having the behaviour.

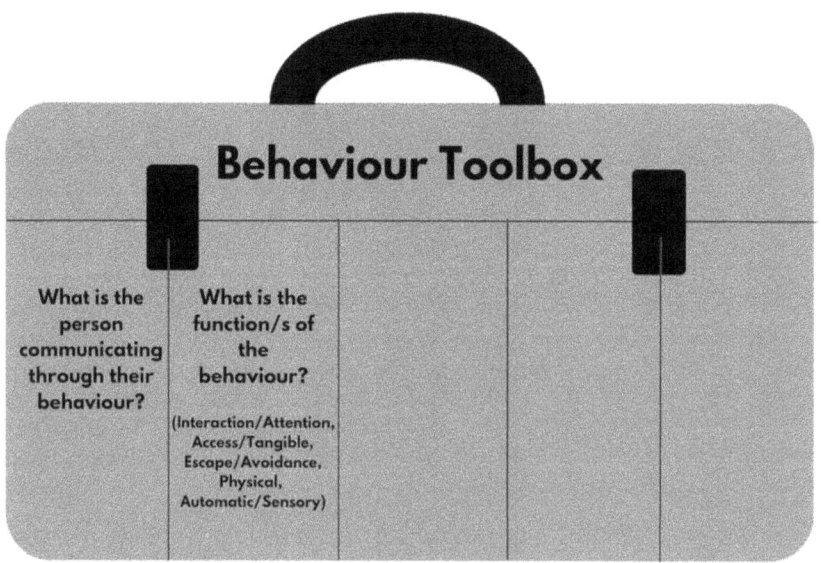

CHAPTER 4

More About the Function of Behaviour

Hopefully by now you are getting a basic handle on what the functions of behaviour are all about. As a recap – there are five functions that any behaviour may fall into:

- **Interaction/attention**
- **Access/tangible**
- **Escape/avoidance**
- **Physical**
- **Automatic/sensory**

In the last chapter, I provided you with some examples of people's behaviour, what they are likely communicating with their behaviour and what the function is. In this chapter I am going to dig a little deeper and provide you with examples that are more complex and creep into some difficult to discuss areas. We are getting to the juicier end of the behaviour spectrum. It will be worth it, I promise! The benefit of analysing more complex behaviours is that we can begin to see that they can serve more than one function.

As a starting point I would like to offer two warnings:

One is a trigger warning. I am going to be discussing intermarital affairs, drinking alcohol, taking drugs, speeding, excessive spending, attending the emergency room repeatedly and bullying. If you have experienced any of these things, I strongly encourage you to seek support for this and if you feel that it is too much, you should skip this chapter. I will not be discussing sexual assault, rape or family violence due to the incredibly sensitive nature of these violent crimes.

Secondly, and this one is a repeat of previous chapters – just because it is a behaviour that is illegal, morally unjust or otherwise undesirable, doesn't mean we can't analyse it and understand it. It by no means implies that I agree with the behaviour or sensationalise the behaviour. I am looking at it with a purely analytical lens and without emotion attached to it. I encourage you to do that same when you start to look at people's behaviour. It makes the process much easier.

Before we get into the examples, I want to share with you a tool we use in our behaviour analysis called the ABC, which stand for:

- A = Antecedent (what was happening directly before the behaviour occurred)
- B = Behaviour (what was the behaviour)
- C = Consequence (what was the consequence of the behaviour or what reinforced the behaviour)

I have added an ABC sheet in the appendix of this book as a starting point if you wish to use this. There are also a broad range of examples available for free on the internet. For the purpose of this chapter, I want you to ignore the 'C' for now. We will discuss that when we get to reinforcement. An ABC sheet might look like this:

Antecedent	Behaviour	Consequence
Jonny and his sister were playing with the toys just prior to lunch and nap time.	Jonny hit his sister with the toy by throwing it at her.	

The reason we use this tool is it is quite useful to look at what was happening just prior to the behaviour. By knowing what was happening prior to the behaviour it gives us insight into what the trigger was or what contributed to the behaviour. **The other important factor at this stage of the book is to know that behaviours are much easier to analyse if you look at single incidents of the behaviour.**

Let's jump in with both feet and look at an intermarital affair.

Example 1 – The affair

A behaviour as old as time is the affair or the relationship that a married or partnered person, who has agreed to a monogamous relationship, engages in. If this has happened to you or if this is something that you have been part of in any way, let's analyse it in general terms. Of course, there are a plethora of additional circumstances that make this situation more complex but you can apply that yourself once we go over the basics. I'm going to use they/them pronouns for most of these more complex examples so that you can apply your own as you choose.

Your friend meets you for a drink and as you get into the conversation, they disclose to you that they have been having an affair outside of their monogamous relationship. You decide to apply the newly found tools you have learnt from this book and so you start thinking about what they are trying to communicate through their behaviour.

Step 1: What are they communicating?

> Answer: There are two answers to this one

1. By telling you about this they are most likely communicating that they need some support or that they are worried about what to do (**Function:** you've probably guessed is interaction)
2. By engaging in the affair, they are communicating any number of things but likely options are: they are unhappy in their relationship, they are seeking stimulation, they are lonely. You know them best and using the ABC tool to help you, you can determine more easily what they are communicating.

Step 2: What is the function of the behaviour? Likely scenarios will depend on their personal situation but for the majority it would be any combination of:

- **Interaction/attention**
- **Access/tangible**
- **Escape/avoidance**

I would suggest that interaction/attention would be involved in any combination. Does that make sense? If you have a personal scenario in mind, I recommend putting it in the ABC chart to see if you can identify the antecedents/triggers.

Example 2 – Drinking alcohol and/or partaking in drug use

For this example, I would like to add that I am not referring to long-term alcohol or drug use that has become an addiction. Addiction is a disease that requires very specific support.

You have been drinking alcohol a lot lately and this has also included some recreational drug use. You decide to apply what you have learnt to your own situation, to reflect the mirror onto yourself, a very brave move. You remember that it is easier to analyse single incidents of behaviour so you think back to last week when you went out to dinner with friends on the Friday night, then to a pub/club afterwards for some drinks and partook in some type of drug while there.

Step 1: What was the behaviour communicating?

> Answer: The behaviour was likely communicating to anyone observing it, that you wanted to have fun with friends and enjoy yourself. There are possibly other things being communicated depending on how far things went or how much you had to drink.

Step 2: What was the function of the behaviour? It is likely to be both **interaction/attention** combined with **escape/avoidance.** Let me explain. If you were to put this in the ABC chart, you might put something in the antecedent column like, 'had just finished working a full week of work' or 'was busy all week with family'.

This would help to reach the conclusion that the function was:

- **Interaction/attention**. As you were needing an interaction with others (your friends) after being busy all week.
- **Escape/avoidance**. As you had a full working week you were likely seeking to escape the stress or memories of the week of work.

If you were to put this in the ABC chart now it might look something like this

Antecedent	Behaviour	Consequence
- Long hard week at work - Busy with family all week	Drinking alcohol and partaking in recreational drug use	You were able to meet the function by gaining interaction with your friends and escaping your surface stress and work memories.

This is not to say that the behaviour you chose is the only way to gain an interaction or escape the stress of work, it's not. It's just the one that you preferred at that time.

Let's look at another one.

Example 3 – Speeding

I wanted to add speeding to this as it is a common behaviour we see and it is one that tends to upset a lot of people. However, it's quite an easy one to analyse.

You are driving along at the speed limit and someone overtakes you doing well over the speed limit. Initially you might react by shaking your head or yelling or swearing. It may not bother you at all. Either way you decide to use your new skills from this book and analyse the behaviour.

Step 1: What is the person communicating through their behaviour?

>Answer: The person may be communicating that they are in a hurry, it may even be an emergency. They may be

More About the Function of Behaviour

communicating that they are going to be late for something. There's probably more they are communicating but without knowing the person it would be hard to know.

Step 2: What is the function of their behaviour? It is both **access/tangible** and **interaction/attention.** I am hoping you were able to guess that one. If you were to put this one into an ABC chart, you might put something into the antecedent column like 'They left it too late to be able to make their appointment in time' or 'They had a flat tyre and had to change it'.

This would help to reach the conclusion that the function was:

- **Access/tangible.** As they were trying to gain access to where they were going in the time frame they had
- **Interaction/attention.** This one was trickier to see in this case but they were gaining a level of attention to their needs which they perceived to be greater than the law.

If you were to put this in the ABC chart now it might look something like this

Antecedent	Behaviour	Consequence
- Did not leave enough time to reach destination - Had a flat tyre so were running late	Speeding	The consequence was possibly one of two things 1. They reached their destination on time, which reinforced the behaviour as meeting their needs 2. They were caught speeding and faced a fine and/or demerit points, which may reduce the behaviour in the future.

In this scenario, the consequence may determine how the behaviour will proceed in the future. However, it may not. Remember I told you about Edward Thorndike in Chapter 1 and his work on law and effect? Punishments don't work well for behaviour modification. They can certainly be satisfying for the person doing the punishing but they gain little in terms of behaviour modification. Positive reinforcers work much better and so a program where a person gained benefits for having a blemish free record on their license would be a better program to put money into. Just a thought.

Example 4 – Excessive Spending

I wanted to touch on this example as it is a common one in our western societies, it also falls into quite a few functions, which I think you will find interesting. I'm going to give you an example but feel free to apply the same principles to your own experience of this or of someone you know. I want to do this one without the ABC chart as I want you to be able to automatically work this out when observing a behaviour. The ABC chart is for when things are a bit murky on the function, as it can help to work it out.

It is payday. The end of a hard week, fortnight or month, depending on your pay cycle. You get home from work and change into comfortable clothes, grab a drink – a coffee or something stronger, and you settle on the couch with your laptop on your knee (this example also works if you have headed straight to the shops or the mall after work). You start browsing and soon you have purchased multiple items that are either in your hands as you carry them to the car or they will arrive in the mail in the next week or two.

Step 1: What are you or the person shopping, trying to communicate through the behaviour?

>Answer: This can be tricky to work out but I want to try. I think the person is communicating that they need some

items for their lives, whether this is a perceived need or an actual need depends on the person and the purchase. They may be communicating that they are seeking an escape from the reality of working or routine. In the case of going to the mall or the shops they may be communicating that they need an interaction with people other than work or family.

Step 2: What is the function of the behaviour? I bet by now you can guess at least one of them. I would say that the function for any kind of excessive spending is both:

- **Access/tangible** (gaining access to desired items)
- **Escape/avoidance** (escaping everyday routine)

I would also suggest that in the case of going to the mall or shops that the function is possibly **interaction/attention** as the person may be needing an interaction from others. In the case of this being a behaviour that occurs every payday or every week, fortnight or month, I would consider that the behaviour falls into the **automatic** function as well. Because it has become an automatic response that meets their needs quite well. Whether this behaviour leaves the person with a lack of money doesn't help with modifying the behaviour. However, now that we know the function, we can consider this when looking for a replacement behaviour to see what will work for modifying the behaviour.

Example 5 – Attending the emergency room or GP repeatedly

I have added this example as I hope that if you come across this scenario with someone that you can look at it with a deeper understanding of their needs.

You know a socially isolated person who regularly attends the emergency room or the GP but is never actually taken into hospital.

They may even be someone who calls an ambulance on a regular basis. However, when they attend the emergency room or the ambulance attends their home, they are taken through all the routine processes of finding out if something is wrong with them medically. This includes having their temperature taken, perhaps a warm blanket on them, and one on one talking to them by a medical staff member. If they attend the GP, they will have some similar experiences. Both scenarios will include talking with an administrative person as well.

You have observed this in someone you know and decide to analyse the behaviour using your skills from this book.

Step 1: What are they trying to communicate through their behaviour?

> Answer: I would think they are trying to communicate that they need an interaction with someone or a meaningful connection with someone. They might be communicating that they are lonely or that they have challenges with maintaining friendships.

Step 2: What is the function of the behaviour? I bet you are guessing these by now. I believe the function is:

- **Interaction/attention** (They are seeking a meaningful connection with others)
- **Access/tangible** (They are seeking access to a different and more supportive environment, possibly even human touch)
- **Physical** (This one could possibly be physical as well due to feelings of loneliness becoming a physical sensation in the body)
- **Automatic** (If this has been happening for a long time it could also be automatic as it has become an effective tool to meet their needs).

More About the Function of Behaviour

This example and the other examples in this chapter are going to feature in the upcoming chapters as we look at replacement behaviour as a means of reducing or modifying the behaviour. So, stay tuned.

Example 6 – Bullying

For this example, I am not going to provide a scenario but instead look at the behaviour of bullying in general. When we talk about bullying, we are talking about targeted behaviour toward someone usually over an extended period of time. However, I think that isolated incidents of being mean to someone actually serves the same function so let's analyse it.

Step 1: What is the person communicating through the behaviour of bullying or being mean to others through their verbal or physical actions?

> Answer: They are communicating that they feel somehow superior to the person they are acting out toward (even though they are not). They are communicating that they want to feel more powerful than the person they are bullying and they are communicating that they want to draw attention away from their own perceived flaws. Sound about right? I am sure there are more than that but it's a starting point.

Step 2: What is the function of the behaviour? Well, there's quite a few depending on the circumstances in which the behaviour occurs. I'd say that the functions are:

- **Attention/interaction** (It may be to gain a level of attention to them. Even if it is negative attention, it is still attention. In fact, negative attention is easier to predict and easier to attain than positive attention)

- **Escape/avoidance** (It could be a way to avoid a task or engaging in an activity or avoid a social interaction they are worried about or may not have the skills to handle. By focusing on you, they avoid having to deal with whatever it is they don't want to deal with)
- **Access/tangible** (This could be true in a workplace where the bully gains access to privileges or activities or money. By highlighting the victim's perceived faults, they inadvertently keep themselves at the top. Some adults become very good at this behaviour and can action it in very strategic ways so it almost goes unnoticed)
- **Automatic** (For some people, there could be a feeling of power, superiority or control that they gain internally through the bullying process, which would unfortunately reinforce the behaviour as meeting a need within them).

One thing I will say about this type of behaviour that I have observed and learnt throughout my life and my career is that it is NEVER about something being wrong with the victim and ALWAYS about something within the perpetrator, such as a function it serves for them.

I am hoping that by the end of this chapter you have gained enough of an insight into the function of behaviours to go out and attempt to analyse at least what the person is communicating and have a guess at what the function of the behaviour might be. Don't worry if it is still unclear in some cases, it will become much easier the more you practise. Don't forget to analyse your own behaviours if you are brave enough.

Toolbox takeaways

- Steps to analysing a person's behaviour are:
    - Step 1: What are they trying to communicate through their behaviour?
    - Step 2: What is the function of the behaviour?
- There are five functions of behaviour – interaction/attention, access/tangible, escape/avoidance, automatic/sensory and physical
- Some behaviours have more than one function
- If you are unclear on what the function might be, use the ABC chart to help.

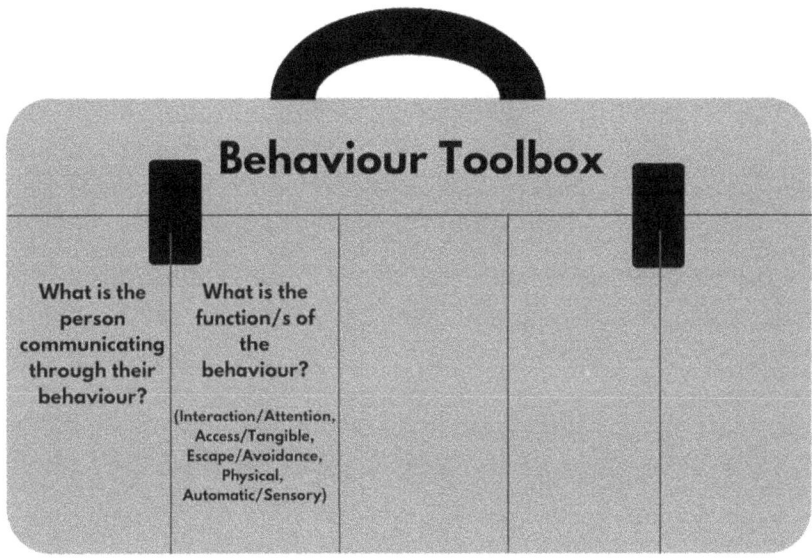

CHAPTER 5

Environment and Reinforcement

OUR ENVIRONMENT IS CRUCIAL IN terms of our everyday interactions and even our survival as a species. Everything about our environment either supports us or hinders us in some way. By environment, I mean both your physical surroundings and the people within it. If you break it down even further then you can observe the more detailed aspects of the environment. These include the people in the environment, the number of people in the environment, cultural factors, the climate, the weather, socioeconomic status, communication style, parenting style, teaching methods, gender, social expectations and much more.

In behaviour analysis and behaviour support, the environment plays a significant role in understanding and analysing a person's behaviour. In fact, the environment plays a crucial role in determining if a behaviour is being reinforced, which means the difference between the behaviour continuing or stopping. As behaviour support practitioners, we spend a great deal of time observing the environment a person has a behaviour in, through actual observations and through discussions with the person or their support people. We do this quite extensively as we are working through an analytical process to create change or modification as well as a nice big chunky report.

My dream for this book has always been to bring what we do as practitioners to you, as an everyday person, in a way that does away with assessments and reports and teaches you to purely use your knowledge to understand behaviour. The likelihood that you will need to write a report on this one day is probably quite low, so let me teach you some basics about the environment that will hopefully stay in your head and be added to your toolbox, so you can easily apply it when trying to understand someone's behaviour. I absolutely know that it is possible to understand a person's behaviour without having extensive assessments otherwise I would not be bringing this to you to apply to your own life. To begin I want to take a look at our toolbox so far.

Behaviour Toolbox				
What is the behaviour you are trying to understand? *Don't forget the ABC chart if you need it*				
What is the person communicating through their behaviour?	What is the function/s of the behaviour? *(Interaction/ attention, access/ tangible, escape/ avoidance, automatic/ sensory, physical)*	What is happening in the environment to reinforce the behaviour?	*Triggers for the behaviour*	*Replacement for the Behaviour*

Environment and Reinforcement

You will see that I have added a third tool to the toolbox and that is, of course, environment. To make it easier, there are three questions I want you to be thinking of asking when you are trying to understand someone's behaviour. These are:

- Who is there?
- Is there something in the physical environment that is contributing to the behaviour?
- What in this environment is keeping the behaviour happening or reinforcing the behaviour?

If you can ask these three questions then you will gain a lot of information about the behaviour itself. Even if, in the moment, you can only think of one of the questions, that's fine too. It's still going to help.

Who is there?

Who is present can mean a lot when a behaviour happens. The person could be someone your person is trying to avoid, trying to impress, is intimidated by, has a trauma history with, has had a relationship with or any number of things. It could be that there are a large number of people there or only a few. It could be that the people there are all a similar age to your person or they may be much older or younger. It could be that all the people there hold positions of power over your person (such as doctors, nurses, teachers, police, other professionals). Whatever the number or the cohort, it really does matter when you are trying to understand behaviour.

People matter because we are inherently social creatures. Without even being aware of it, we are all constantly scanning our environments for safety and threat. By scanning the environment and knowing who is in it, it helps us to predict the environment we are in and if we can predict it, we can reduce our anxiety or fear about that environment. Walking into an environment made up of only family members or people we know and trust is vastly different to walking into an environment with strangers. You can mostly predict the behaviour of people you know and but you absolutely cannot know or trust the people who are strangers. This is why it can be exhausting to spend the day in a new or unfamiliar environment. It is therefore really helpful to have a predictable environment but we'll talk about this in later chapters where I delve into strategies for managing behaviour.

The following are some examples of having different people in an environment impacting on behaviour.

- Your child arrives home from school and has a behaviour with only you there. This is due to you being a predictable person in their life and also a 'repairable' relationship. They have most likely been managing their behaviour all day amongst their teachers and their peers, none of whom they can predict as well as they can predict you. They feel safe to let it all out with only you in the environment.
- Your partner arrives home from work and stomps about angrily after having to deal with an office full of people all day. Again, you are a predictable person (well on most days I am) and most likely a repairable relationship.
- Your friend is out with you and starts behaving very differently when their ex-partner enters the establishment. Their behaviour initially was based on the relationship between the two of you. By adding another person to that environment, their relationship and history with the other person can change the dynamic of the situation.
- You witness a person behaving pretty wildly at the local pub, shouting and swearing, which changes significantly when two police officers turn up looking for someone else.
- You drop your teenager off to meet up with their friends and you observe their behaviour as they walk off with

Environment and Reinforcement

them and you notice that it is very different to how they behave around you.

The list is endless. The people around the behaviour matter, so ask the question of 'Who is there?' if you can, when you are trying to understand a person's behaviour.

Is there something in the physical environment contributing to the behaviour?

Looking at the physical environment is just as useful as knowing who was in the environment. The reason for this is that every environment has unwritten rules and we are supposed to know them all and adhere to them. I once took one of our children to a live football match with my husband. It was their first live match in a huge stadium with a lot of people. Once the game started, my husband yelled out some kind of encouragement (ahem, criticism) to the umpires. This particular child has a lot of social anxiety and so they turned to me and quietly said, 'Mum, can you *please* ask dad to not yell out things like that, I'm really embarrassed.' I quickly explained that at a football game it's socially acceptable to yell out things and that if they waited a few minutes, they would see that most other people would be doing the same. They watched for a while and then said to me 'I'll allow it', jokingly of course. The point being that once they knew the social rules of the environment, they were comfortable and their anxiety reduced. Their father continued to yell out and cheer and all was well, except that their team lost. But that's a whole other book about tolerating distress.

The physical environment can tell us a lot about the person's behaviour and so observing it can be a really useful thing to do when asking yourself the question of what in the physical environment is contributing to the behaviour. Is the room too hot, too cold, is there a ceiling fan that's blowing on them and irritating them, at work is there a huge aircon system that rumbles continuously, are they stuck in a small cabin of a truck all day, is the environment one they have never been in before (first time at a dentist), is there someone in their environment who is not usually there, is the room too noisy, too crowded, too stuffy, are people confined to their seats for a long plane ride ...?

To unpack this one, it can be useful to try two different ways to find what is happening in the environment: you can ask the person if anything in the room was uncomfortable or bothering them, *or* you can observe the room or the physical environment yourself. If you are observing the environment yourself, try to make note of how your person interacts within the room or the space they are in. Look at how they move, what they notice, where they sit, where they stand, if they seem comfortable, if they seem irritated. This will help you in analysing the physical environment alongside temperature and the other things I mentioned at the start of this chapter.

The following are some examples of how a physical environment can impact on behaviour.

- Your person is a tradie and used to being in environments that are more casual. You have to attend a formal meeting at your child's school. Your partner modifies his behaviour to be different in this environment than on the worksite.
- You are on a plane, heading somewhere amazing. However, you are confined to your seat and three rows back there is a baby crying. Three rows in front there is a toddler constantly asking questions. It makes you feel really irritable and you get snappy with your friend. I shouldn't blame the children, but hey, we've all been on a flight like this!
- You are on a holiday in far north Queensland or another tropical location where the humidity is stifling. Even though the location is beautiful, you find yourself becoming irritable due to the humidity.
- Relaxing at home, long weekend, chilling on the couch, no pressures, you easily remain cool, calm and collected.

Environment and Reinforcement

- It's nighttime and you have to walk home in the dark, through a darkened street, your phone has gone flat and there is no-one around. This environment impacts on your behaviour. You are on alert; your hearing is heightened and it is much more obvious that you are scanning your environment for safety and risk.

Environment matters. And physical environment matters. Have a go at identifying some different environments that you think contribute to behaviours.

What in this environment is keeping the behaviour happening or reinforcing the behaviour?

This is a question that will really help when trying to find replacements for the behaviours you want to lessen or stop. There is a really important thing you should know. A behaviour cannot exist or remain without something reinforcing it. Let me say it again so you remember this key point.

> **A behaviour cannot exist or remain without something reinforcing it.**

For a behaviour to exist at all it has come into contact with a reinforcer. What do I mean by a reinforcer? I mean that something has occurred in response to the behaviour that has made the person feel it is worth having that behaviour again. For example, let's go back to our young person in the second chapter, who went to the supermarket with her parent and requested an Xbox gaming pass voucher. The mum initially said no to this request but then the daughter was quiet, didn't speak and was a little bit sad looking. She then requested to go and sit in the car to wait for her parent to finish the shopping. What if after the daughter went to the car, the parent starting to feel guilty, then justified the purchase and ended up adding it to the grocery order and surprising the teenager with it?

Without us judging this behaviour, we can see that the purchase of the item reinforced the behaviour of 'sulking'. You see what I mean? Now that's not to say that you should never buy your child something they want. But there's a way to teach this that means you won't have the same behaviour every time they want something that you have previously said no to.

What about the child from Chapter 2, who arrived at school, to discover they had a maths class and so hid in the toilets to avoid the class? What if they were never found out that they had missed the class, or if the house head had not made contact with the parent to address the behaviour? The behaviour would have been reinforced as meeting their need. It would then feel like a really good strategy to try next time there was something challenging at school that they didn't want to face. If this worked time and time again, it could set the pattern for the behaviour as being a really good one to use throughout life whenever something hard came along.

What about drinking alcohol? What is the reinforcer for using alcohol as a means of interaction or escaping stress? The reinforcer is the endorphins that flood through you when you drink alcohol. Which are quite strong. Strong enough that even the threat of possibly feeling quite crappy the next day is not an adequate deterrent. The endorphins reinforce that the behaviour of drinking alcohol (and drugs too) is a good choice for you to make at the time and meets the need you have. So, you are much more likely to do it again.

Excessive shopping and spending of money is very similar. The reinforcer is even stronger as not only do you have it reinforced through the initial purchase with a rush of endorphins, you get to have the item and keep it, which reinforces it even further. Again, when you use it for the first time or wear it for the first time. It's reinforced again and again until it wears off. Have you ever wondered why you like to go and look at or hold new purchases? I remember one time when my husband had bought himself a new (second hand) trail motorbike. He'd put it away in the garage and then later that night he laughingly said, 'I'm just going to go out and look at my motorbike again', and while we both chuckled, he did indeed go and look at it again, no doubt checking the various components and enjoying the endorphins associated with it and with the anticipation of taking it for a ride the next day. When it comes to these types of reinforcers though, as we gain a few experiences over the years, we discover that the 'feel good' endorphins eventually fade and we start to see that this behaviour is not actually meeting the need any more or for long enough. Pity. Because these things can be fun!

My point in these examples is that you need to be looking for what is reinforcing the behaviour enough that it makes it continue to be the behaviour that the person uses over and above other behaviours to meet the need they have. And to meet the function! Let's not forget that the behaviour is meeting one of the five functions of interaction/attention, access/tangible, escape/avoidance, automatic and physical. On this point, you will find that with the functions of automatic or physical, there is less likely to be a reinforcer within the environment. This is because the function comes from within the person and not from the environment. Let me explain this a little further. With our example in earlier chapters of tapping fingernails on the counter or even cracking knuckles, it was driven from a need inside the person, due to how it felt within them. So, it's therefore going to be less likely to be reinforced from the environment and much more likely to be reinforced from how it felt and the relief it gave them.

The question I want you to make sure you ask is 'What is making the behaviour happen or what is keeping the behaviour happening?'. If you can answer that, then you have your reinforcer. When we get to the chapter of replacement behaviours and the chapter on strategies, I will expand on reinforcers much more and look at how to use them to find ways to reduce or stop behaviours in others and yourself.

Toolbox takeaways

- Steps to analysing a person's behaviour are:
    - Step 1: What are they trying to communicate through their behaviour?
    - Step 2: What is the function of the behaviour?
    - Step 3: What is happening in the environment?
- There are five functions of behaviour – interaction/attention, access/tangible, escape/avoidance, automatic/sensory and physical.
- Understanding the environment can help to understand the behaviour.
- Ask yourself three key questions about the environment:
    - Who is there?
    - Is there something in the physical environment that is contributing to the behaviour?
    - What in this environment is keeping the behaviour happening or reinforcing the behaviour?
- Look for the reinforcers of the behaviour.
- Remember: **A behaviour cannot exist or remain without something reinforcing it.**

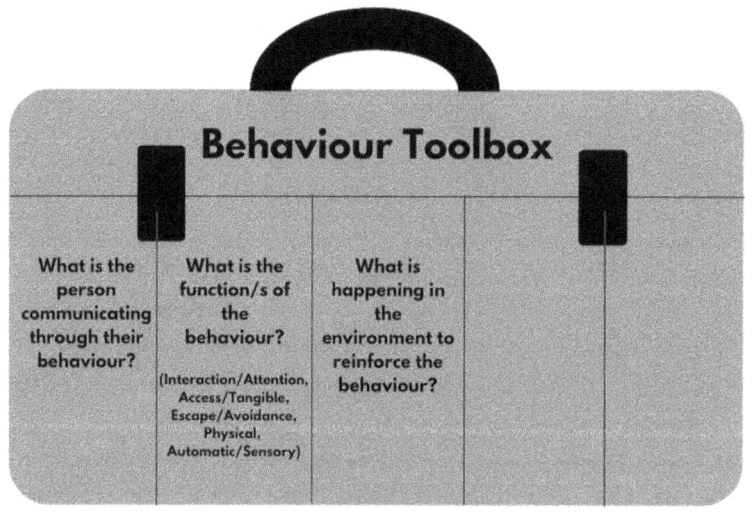

CHAPTER 6

Triggers

TRIGGER HAS BECOME A MUCH more widely used term in the last decade, supported by those who are in touch with their feelings and emotions and the things that really tick them off. It is a word that is now readily used for describing something that triggered an emotion, usually used in a negative context. When I was growing up not as many people were in touch with their feelings, so the only time you heard the word trigger was in relation to the mechanisms of a gun. Society has come far in a short period of time.

In behaviour support and behaviour analysis, the term trigger refers to something that has happened prior to the behaviour occurring that is directly related to it. We even break it down further to what are called setting events and triggers. Essentially, setting events could be described as slower triggers. They 'set the stage' on which the behaviour will happen if there is a fast trigger. However, a behaviour can occur from a setting event OR a trigger. It is just that there is much more likely to be a behaviour if you have both a setting event AND a trigger. These are both what is referred to when talking about an antecedent in Chapter 4. The antecedent is the thing that happens just before the behaviour. When we talk about an antecedent we are talking about triggers.

Examples of setting events include: feeling sad around Christmas time, challenges with receptive and expressive language, grieving for a loved one, sleeping difficulties, a lot of stress at work, constant noise from having three very young children, the list goes on and is different for every person and often different for each behaviour. As behaviour support practitioners we don't usually add medical conditions to this list as we would refer to them as more 'predisposing factors' that contribute to the behaviour. Someone might have tinnitus or treatment for cancer and that would be a predisposing factor that could possibly impact on behaviour.

Examples of triggers include: someone yelling at you, someone taking something from you, someone pushing you, something breaking that you were needing, hurting yourself in some way like stubbing your toe, money being missing from your account. The list is almost endless and just like setting events the list is different for every person and often different for each behaviour.

The two types of antecedents work together and I'll explain how. Let's say that you have a lot of stress happening at work at the moment and you get to your car to go home and your car has broken down. The two events are much more likely to cause a behaviour like you yelling and swearing than if work was not at all stressful and your car broke down. Make sense? The same for when you are grieving for someone you love and then amongst that some money is missing from your bank account. Your behaviour is going to be different than if money was suddenly missing from your bank account during a time of happiness.

Setting events and triggers can actually be quite challenging to separate from each other and for that reason (and because I believe that understanding behaviour works just as well using purely triggers), I am going to use only the term triggers to describe antecedents from this point forward. Outside of a clinical setting the term 'trigger' is more than adequate to describe what has occurred and to help understand what caused the behaviour. I merely wanted you to gain an understanding that there are different types of triggers that you might come across and some are slower and some are faster. It is useful to know this if you are ever reading additional material about behaviour too. For now, let's take a look at our toolbox and the tools we have added.

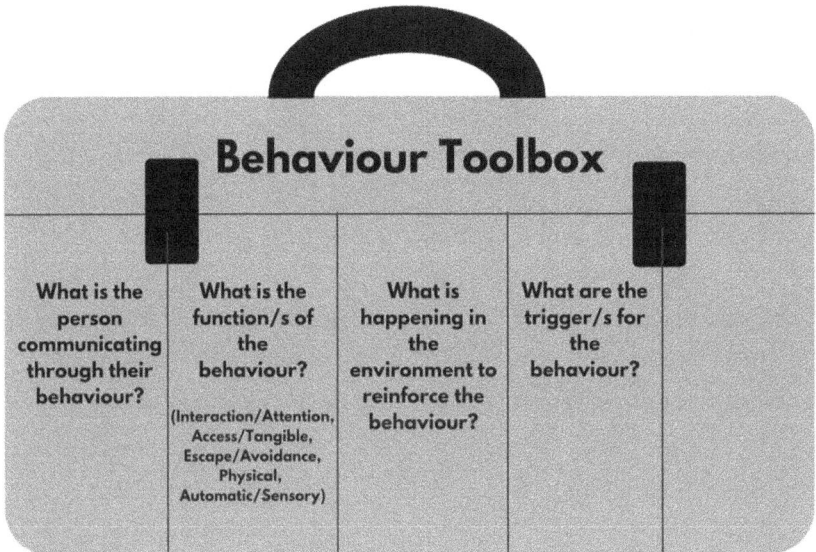

You can see that I have added triggers to the tools in your toolbox and while we could have spoken about this in earlier chapters, I deliberately left it until now so that it is straight after the chapter about environment. The reason for this is that by assessing the environment you will work out what the trigger is for the behaviour. The trigger also works nicely into the ABC chart if you use this. I would change the acronym to be trigger instead of antecedent but then it would be the TBC chart and I don't want to confuse things. Instead, I will change it to the following:

Antecedent/Trigger	Behaviour	Consequence/Reinforcer
Stressful week at work. Needing to unwind	Spent a lot of money on online shopping	Endorphins from the purchase and the package arriving
Friends had access to cooler features than them. Saw the vouchers in the supermarket	Sulking in the supermarket when parent would not buy the voucher the teenager wanted	Parent bought the voucher, which reinforced the behaviour
Grieving for parent. Money missing from bank account	Yelled at partner for excessively spending money from bank account	Gained the space they were looking for as the partner left the house, so it was an effective tool to meet the needs. Well, initially anyway

You will see that I have also changed the 'consequence' column to add 'reinforcer', which is a more accurate description of what you are looking for when trying to understand someone's behaviour. I have added some of the examples we have been discussing to show you how the ABC chart can be used to make what is happening clearer. It becomes clearer when you look at the examples in the ABC chart above that we can combine the slow and the fast triggers and apply them as just triggers.

The environment, the behaviour and even the reinforcer gives us enough information to be able to work out what the trigger or triggers are for each behaviour. Working out the function can also give us a clue. They all work together to form one big picture about the behaviour and if we have one big picture then we can find a way to lessen, remove, modify or stop the behaviour. Especially if we have a willing candidate.

Triggers

The other reason for working out the triggers for a behaviour is that it can help us know when the behaviour is more likely to happen again. It can then help us to be able to predict behaviours.

Now that we have the fourth step in our process, let's take another look at our examples from previous chapters and apply the formula up to this stage.

Example 1 – Attending the emergency room or GP repeatedly

Remember from this example, you have a socially isolated person who regular attends the emergency room or the GP but is never actually taken into hospital. They may even be someone who calls an ambulance on a regular basis. However, when they attend the emergency room or the ambulance attends their home, they are taken through all the routine processes of finding out if something is wrong with them medically. This includes having their temperature taken, perhaps a warm blanket on them, one on one talking to them by a medical staff member. If they attend the GP, they will have some similar experiences. Both scenarios will include talking with an administrative person as well.

You have observed this in someone you know and decide to analyse the behaviour using your skills from this book.

Step 1: What are they trying to communicate through their behaviour?

> Answer: We established that they are trying to communicate that they need an interaction with someone or a meaningful connection with someone and that they might be communicating that they are lonely or that they have challenges with maintaining friendships.

Step 2: What is the function of the behaviour? We worked out that the function was most likely:

- **Interaction/attention** (They are seeking a meaningful connection with others)
- **Access/tangible** (They are seeking access to a different and more supportive environment, possibly even human touch)
- **Physical** (This one could possibly be physical as well due to feelings of loneliness becoming a physical sensation in the body)
- **Automatic** (If this has been happening for a long time it could also be automatic as it has become an effective tool to meet their needs)

Step 3: Environment

Ask yourself the question: **What is happening in the environment to reinforce the behaviour?**

- **Who is there?** (At home there is probably no-one there, we can ask the person this question to find out)
- **Is there something in the physical environment contributing to the behaviour?** (Yes, their physical environment is most likely lonely and the new environment provides stimulation)
- **What in this environment is keeping the behaviour happening or reinforcing the behaviour?** (It is being reinforced from the behaviour meeting their need or the function of interaction/attention)

Step 4: Trigger

Ask yourself the question: **What is the likely trigger for this behaviour?** While being careful to not make harmful assumptions, I would begin by having a conversation with the person and if possible, with those supporting them. For this example, you have had a conversation with the person and you have discovered the following:

- They are very lonely
- It is often happening on the off week to when they go into the community to do shopping
- This started when they lost their drivers licence, which made them more socially isolated.

You see how by applying the steps we gain a lot of information about what is happening around the behaviour. In the next chapter we are going to take this example to the final step of replacement behaviour.

Let's do another one.

Example 2 – Excessive spending

It is payday. The end of a hard week, fortnight or month, depending on your pay cycle. You get home from work and change into comfortable clothes, grab a drink – a coffee or something stronger, and you settle on the couch with your laptop on you knee (this example also works if you have headed straight to the shops or the mall after work). You start browsing and soon you have purchased multiple items that are either in your hands as you carry them to the car or they will arrive in the mail in the next week or two.

Step 1: What are you or the person shopping, trying to communicate through the behaviour?

>Answer: We established that the person is communicating that they need some items for their lives, whether this is a perceived need or an actual need depends on the person and the purchase. We also established that they are communicating that they are seeking an escape from

the reality of working or routine. In the case of going to the mall or the shops they may be communicating that they need an interaction with people other than work or family. For the purpose of understanding this behaviour and the steps we will stick with online shopping. Remember I spoke earlier about it being easier if we analyse each behaviour individually?

Step 2: What is the function of the behaviour? We established that the function was both:

- **Access/tangible** (gaining access to desired items)
- **Escape/avoidance** (escaping everyday routine)

Step 3: Environment

Ask yourself the question: **What is happening in the environment to reinforce the behaviour?**

- **Who is there?** (In this case they are alone at home, which is significant as it adds to the escape function. They are gaining an escape from the people at work.)
- **Is there something in the physical environment contributing to the behaviour?** (Yes, their physical environment has been set up by them to support comfort, changing into comfortable clothing, laptop on lap, drink in hand AND it's easily accessible.)
- **What in this environment is keeping the behaviour happening or reinforcing the behaviour?** (It is being reinforced by the endorphins from online shopping and purchasing items and it is being reinforced by the packages arriving. It is also meeting the functions of the behaviour, which is access/tangible and escape/avoidance)

Step 4: Trigger

Ask yourself the question: **What is the likely trigger for this behaviour?** If this was our own behaviour, we could ask ourselves what is happening right before this behaviour is occurring and if this was someone we know we could have the same conversation with them, if they were open to it. In this instance the likely triggers would be:

- Long hard week at work
- Payday
- Environment set up for easy access to online shopping
- Perceived or real need of items.

You see how by knowing the triggers in this situation we can easily predict when the behaviour is most likely to occur again? This is important and we will touch on this in the next chapter when we look at replacement behaviours.

Let's do one more.

Example 3 – Gossiping

I'm going to look at gossiping for our final behaviour and use an example similar to the one in Chapter 3.

You find out that a co-worker has been gossiping about you, making up rumours and saying generally unkind things to others. You are really confused as you thought that they were your work friend and the behaviour really upsets you. However, you decide to analyse the behaviour using your newly acquired skills.

Step 1: What were they trying to communicate?

> Answer: We established that they were trying to communicate that they know something about you that no-one else does,

therefore they feel socially superior in that moment with whoever they are sharing the information with.

Step 2: We then established that the function of the behaviour is **interaction/attention** and we considered that by talking about you behind your back they are actually seeking to make a deeper connection with those they are talking with. It gives them a sense of social superiority and actually enhances their connection and acceptance in the group or relationship.

Step 3: Environment

Ask yourself the question: **What is happening in the environment to reinforce the behaviour?**

- **Who is there?** (Other people are there and they are gaining an interaction with them based on their shared knowledge of you.)
- **Is there something in the physical environment contributing to the behaviour?** (Yes, often when people work in shared environments, they seek out others to connect with.)
- **What in this environment is keeping the behaviour happening or reinforcing the behaviour?** (This behaviour is being reinforced by others becoming interested in what the person is saying. If each person they spoke with walked away instead of listening then the behaviour would lessen.)

Step 4: Trigger

Ask yourself the question: **What is the likely trigger for this behaviour?** Hmm, this is a trickier one as the trigger is most likely something within them. Possibly a predisposing factor. But that could be combined with the following:

- Loneliness
- Challenges in making and maintaining friends (lowered social intelligence)
- Environment set up for easy access to people who will listen consistently.

As you can see from this behaviour, we can make some guesses about the triggers without making full blown assumptions. We can't really ask the person what their triggers are without some kind of confrontation (which would likely not give you any accurate information). But sometimes understanding the WHY of a behaviour, makes it easier to just leave it alone.

One final point

The final thing you need to know about triggers is that even if you can't see what the trigger is, there is always a trigger. However, keep in mind that a trigger can be something that is really small or be something internal for the person. Working out the trigger is not essential to finding a replacement for the behaviour but it does help in forming the overall broad picture and it helps to predict when the behaviour might happen again. In the next chapter we look at what we can do about the behaviour. Exciting!

Toolbox takeaways

- Steps to analysing a person's behaviour are:
    - Step 1: What are they trying to communicate through their behaviour?
    - Step 2: What is the function of the behaviour?
    - Step 3: What is happening in the environment?
    - Step 4: What is the trigger?
- A trigger is the antecedent or the thing that happens before the behaviour happens.
- By knowing the trigger, you can predict when a behaviour will be more likely to happen again.
- You can now apply Steps 1-4 in the process of understanding a person's behaviour.
- **There is ALWAYS a trigger even if it is not obvious – you just have to work it out.**

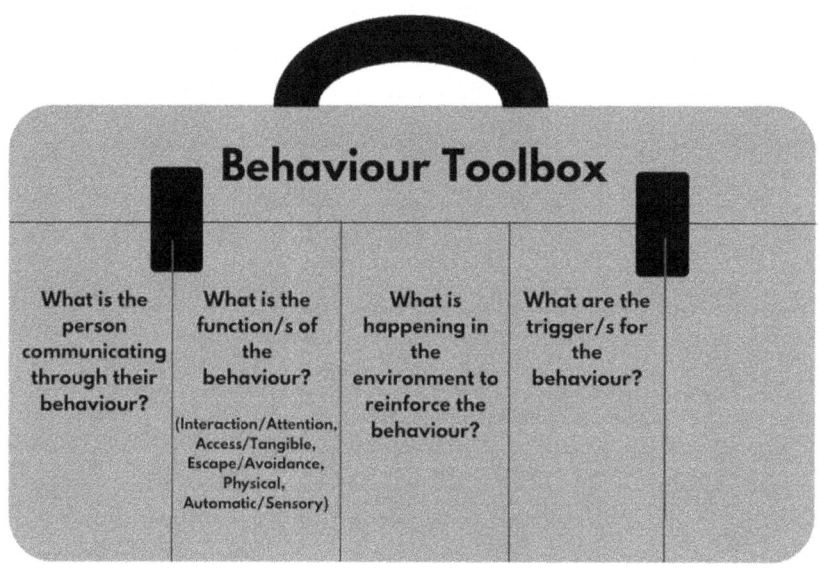

CHAPTER 7

Replacement Behaviours

IN THE WORLD OF BEHAVIOUR support we are called upon to develop what are called functionally equivalent replacement behaviours (or FERB for short) which is a long-winded way of saying a replacement behaviour. The functionally equivalent part is all about what we should be focusing on when looking for a replacement behaviour. The function. But let me explain why.

In order to change, reduce, modify, stop or even influence a behaviour, the most effective way is to replace it with a different behaviour that meets the same function of the behaviour we are trying to change. We learnt in Chapter 1 from Thorndike that a **positive reinforcement is more effective at increasing a desired behaviour than a punishment is of decreasing an undesirable behaviour.** What is even more effective is replacing the behaviour with one that has the same function. We spent two chapters going over the function of behaviour and for good reason. If we know the function, we can change the behaviour.

Any behaviour you are trying to decrease should have a replacement behaviour you are trying to increase. This is true of everyone: adults, children and adolescents.

However, you can't just stop a behaviour and do nothing else as that is merely an *absence* of behaviour. This won't set you up to see effective change. The first thing you need to ask yourself is:

'What do I want them to do instead?' or 'What do I want to see instead?'

Let me give you a couple of basic examples, I'm going to use children for the first couple of examples as that is easier for demonstrating strategies.

Example 1

Your toddler is banging their toy on the window right next to where you are working. You have worked through the four steps:

- Step 1: What are they trying to communicate through their behaviour?
- Step 2: What is the function of the behaviour?
- Step 3: What is happening in the environment?
- Step 4: What is the trigger?

You have determined that they are trying to communicate that they need an interaction, the function is **interaction/attention**, the environment is just you and them and it seems that the trigger is likely boredom or loneliness. What is the replacement behaviour?

Replacement Behaviours

The replacement behaviour can be worked out in the following way:

- You think to yourself, **'What do I want them to do instead?'** The answer is that you want them to play with the toy appropriately and you want them to learn to ask you when they need your attention.
- You then do the following:
    - You say, 'It looks like you need me right now. You can say "please play with me" or "please help me".' (whichever suits your situation)
    - You are also going to model the behaviour you are wanting to see. So, you demonstrate an appropriate way to play with the toy.
- The key to this is that every time the child requests you play with them, while you are teaching this replacement behaviour, or asks for your help, you provide it as much as you can. **This then provides a reinforcement for the new behaviour.**

Example 2

Your teenager walks off and refuses to do their chore, let's say it's emptying the dishwasher. You have worked through the four steps:

- Step 1: What are they trying to communicate through their behaviour?
- Step 2: What is the function of the behaviour?
- Step 3: What is happening in the environment?
- Step 4: What is the trigger?

You have worked out that they are communicating that they don't want to do this job right now, but obviously you want them to follow the house rules. You feel that the function of the behaviour is **escape**. The environment is busy with the whole family there and you feel that the trigger was their brother flicking them with the tea towel causing pain and annoyance. What is the replacement behaviour?

The replacement behaviour can be worked out I the following way:

- Again, ask yourself, **'What do I want them to do instead?'** and of course it is to empty the dishwasher. But you are also aware that you don't want the situation to blow up into a huge drama where everyone gets upset. The other thing you want them to do is to communicate with you and work out a solution.
- You then do the following:
    - You follow them to their room, obviously keeping your cool
    - You say to them, 'I can see you're upset with what happened, I will take care of that for you. How about you come out later and finish the job when your brother/sister is not there? Next time, please just say to me, I need a break from this. I'll come back later'.
- The key again to this is that next time this happens and they request some time, you grant it and say 'I appreciate that you asked'.

I understand that these are both very idealistic behaviours and reactions and that in everyday life it may not go down this smoothly but persevere. You may be surprised at the results.

Now that we've reached the replacement behaviour tool, let's take a look at the toolbox.

Replacement Behaviours

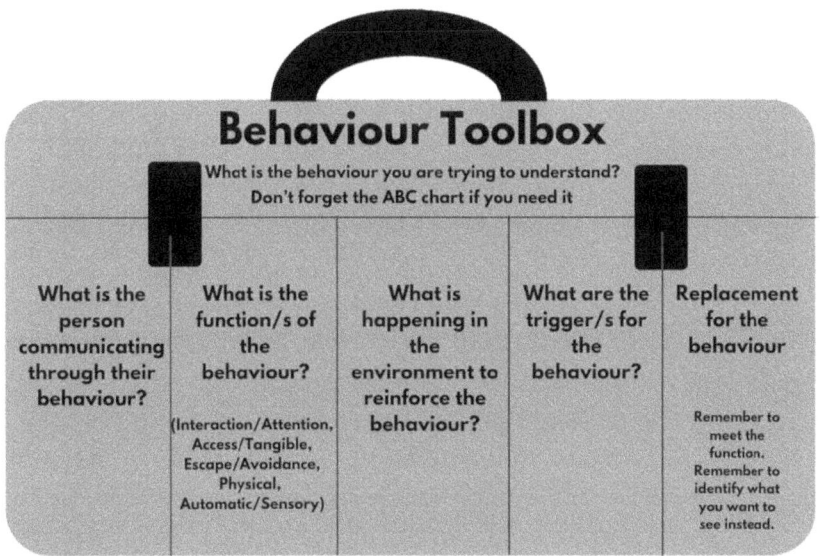

You are probably thinking to yourself at this point, that's all well and good for children, who you have some control over, but what about adults who are not going to follow your instructions or go along with what we want them to do? That is a very good question and the answer is ... somewhat the same. Let me explain.

You are obviously not going to be able to apply *exactly* the same method outlined above to some random person in your workplace. But using similar principles you should be able to guide the behaviour. I'll give you a couple of examples.

Example 1

You are on a building site and one of the newer recruits keeps taking your tools, using them without asking and then leaving them laying all over the site. You are becoming more and more angry about it and initially, you think about confronting him at lunch and ripping him to shreds about his behaviour. But you suddenly remember to apply what you have learned in this book to the situation. You work through the process and realise the function is **access/tangible.** You also realise that he probably doesn't know the workplace 'rules' yet (remember, I talked about every environment having a set of social rules that apply?). You decide on a plan to test out this theory.

You work out the replacement behaviour in the following way:

- You ask yourself what behaviour you want to see instead, likely it's that he asks you if he can use your tools, and that he returns it to the same place he borrowed it from and in the same order as he found them
- You take him aside one morning and say 'Bill, I'm not sure if you know the rules here but from now on, I'd like you to come and ask me if you can borrow my tools and then if I'm happy to lend them to you, you return them how you found them. Understand?' Let's assume it's a perfect world and he says, 'No worries, mate, I didn't realise they were yours.'
- The next stage is the crucial stage. The reinforcer. Every time he asks to borrow the tools you try to say yes. Obviously only if it actually suits you and you're not using the tool he wants. But then you add, 'Appreciate you asking Bill' and then leave it at that. You could even reinforce the return of the tools by saying, 'Appreciate you returning them how you found them' or something like that.

You see how you can influence those around you and their behaviour by using a few strategies? All without them even knowing what you are doing.

Let's look at another work one.

Example 2

Your boss consistently asks you to complete tasks late in the day making it an almost impossible task for you to finish by the end of

Replacement Behaviours

the day deadline. You have gone through the process of working out the behaviour and have established that the function is most likely **access/tangible** and possibly automatic as it seems that they don't even realise that they are doing this to you. You decide on a plan to test out this theory.

You work out the replacement behaviour in the following way:

- IF you have a good working relationship with them you request that they bring additional tasks to you prior to a set time that would allow you to complete the tasks with better results than if you are limited
- You give no reaction to the tasks that are being brought to you late in the day, initially, so as to not reinforce the behaviour
- You set up a time to check in with them each day at a set time, such as 1pm and you ask if they have any additional tasks for you. Thereby setting up a boundary and modelling the behaviour you want to see in them
- Each time they bring you a task early, you say to them, 'I really appreciate that you've brought this to me so early. It gives me plenty of time to do the job well' which reinforces it as they receive this praise each time you see the behaviour.

Over time this will see the boss modify their behaviour. Unless of course you have a particularly challenging boss, which can take a lot longer.

You see how you can influence people using these skills? You can also easily influence a whole office of people using these skills.

For the last half of this chapter, I want to bring forward some of the examples from other chapters so that you can see the entire process at work, culminating in a replacement behaviour.

Example 1 – Attending the emergency room or GP repeatedly

This is the one about the socially isolated person who regular attends the emergency room or the GP but is never actually taken into hospital.

Step 1: We established that they are trying to communicate that they need an interaction with someone or a meaningful connection with someone and that they might be communicating that they are lonely or that they have challenges with maintaining friendships.

Step 2: We worked out that the function was most likely:

- **Interaction/attention** (They are seeking a meaningful connection with others)
- **Access/tangible** (They are seeking access to a different and more supportive environment, possibly even human touch)
- **Physical** (This one could possibly be physical as well due to feelings of loneliness becoming a physical sensation in the body)
- **Automatic** (If this has been happening for a long time it could also be automatic as it has become an effective tool to meet their needs)

But the most prevalent one was **interaction/attention**.

Step 3: We asked, '**What is happening in the environment to reinforce the behaviour?**'

- **Who is there?** (At home there is probably no-one there, we can ask the person this question to find out.)
- **Is there something in the physical environment contributing to the behaviour?** (Yes, their physical environment is most likely lonely and the new environment provides stimulation.)
- **What in this environment is keeping the behaviour happening or reinforcing the behaviour?** (It is being reinforced from the

Replacement Behaviours

behaviour meeting their need or the function of interaction/attention.)

Step 4: We established that the most likely triggers were:

- They are very lonely
- It is often happening on the off week to when they go into the community to do shopping
- This started when they lost their drivers licence, which made them more socially isolated.

Step 5: Replacement behaviours

- We are going to set up a replacement person for them to call when they are needing an interaction. You set this up through your local community house, exploring in the process if there are any social groups you could link them in with. You also set them up with access through the community car. Having someone check in with them once a week for a catch up will help to provide a reinforcer for the new behaviours. This will hopefully lead to the person only attending the GP or emergency room when they have an actual physical issue.

Example 2 – Excessive spending

This is our person who heads straight to the mall or shops online every payday.

Step 1: We established that the person is communicating that they need some items for their lives, whether this is a perceived need or an actual need depends on the person and the purchase. We also established that they are communicating that they are seeking an escape from the reality of working or routine. In the case of going to the mall or the shops they may be communicating that they need an interaction with people other than work or family. For the purpose of understanding this behaviour and the steps we will stick with online shopping.

Step 2: We established that the function was both:

- **Access/tangible** (gaining access to desired items)
- **Escape/avoidance** (escaping everyday routine).

Step 3: We asked the question, 'What is happening in the environment to reinforce the behaviour?'

- **Who is there?** (In this case they are alone at home, which is significant as it adds to the escape function. They are gaining an escape from the people at work.)
- **Is there something in the physical environment contributing to the behaviour?** (Yes, their physical environment has been set up by them to support comfort, changing into comfortable clothing, laptop on lap, drink in hand AND it's easily accessible.)
- **What in this environment is keeping the behaviour happening or reinforcing the behaviour?** (It is being reinforced by the endorphins from online shopping and purchasing items and it is being reinforced by the packages arriving. It is also meeting the functions of the behaviour, which is access/tangible and escape/avoidance).

Step 4: We established that the triggers were:

- Long hard week at work
- Payday
- Environment set up for easy access to online shopping
- Perceived or real need of items.

Step 5: Replacement behaviours

- We are going to look at other ways to achieve the feeling of **escape/avoidance** at the end of the work week – this might be meeting with friends, going to a movie, hiring a movie at home, which would still give the cosy feeling of comfortable clothing and a blanket. If this is you, then look at ways to meet the function for yourself.

- The other function is **access/tangible**. Obviously, you still need some things in your life and I'm not saying to never buy yourself anything. What I'm saying is that if this has become a problem for you, then maybe it could use some modifications. Such as setting limit on the amount you spend for **access/tangible** driven purchases. Or making it that you have to 'sleep on it' for three nights minimum for any purchase over $500 (or whatever limit suits you). But you will find, and I talk about this in Chapter 9, that once you notice the pattern of the behaviour, you will be less likely to engage in it.

Example 3 – Gossiping

I'm going to look at gossiping for our final behaviour and use an example similar to the one in Chapter 3.

You find out that a co-worker has been gossiping about you, making up rumours and saying generally unkind things to others. You are really confused as you thought that they were your work friend and the behaviour really upsets you. However, you decide to analyse the behaviour using your newly acquired skills.

Step 1: We established that they were trying to communicate that they know something about you that no-one else does, therefore they feel socially superior in that moment with whoever they are sharing the information with.

Step 2: We then established that the function of the behaviour is **interaction/attention** and we considered that by talking about you behind your back they are actually seeking to make a deeper connection with those they are talking with. It gives them a sense of social superiority and actually enhances their connection and acceptance in the group or relationship.

Step 3: We asked the question, 'What is happening in the environment to reinforce the behaviour?'

- **Who is there?** (Other people are there and they are gaining an interaction with them based on their shared knowledge of you.)
- **Is there something in the physical environment contributing to the behaviour?** (Yes, often when people work in shared environments, they seek out others to connect with.)
- **What in this environment is keeping the behaviour happening or reinforcing the behaviour?** (This behaviour is being reinforced by others becoming interested in what the person is saying. If each person they spoke with walked away instead of listening then the behaviour would lessen.)

Step 4: We established that the triggers were possibly:

- Loneliness
- Challenges in making and maintaining friends (lowered social intelligence)
- Environment set up for easy access to people who will listen consistently.

Step 5: Replacement behaviours

You ask yourself, 'What do I want them to do instead?' And the answer is likely that you want them to leave you alone. But beneath that, you want them to reduce their gossiping behaviour and increase their conversations about other things, such as work, TV shows, music, whatever you think.

In order to see a decrease in this behaviour, every time they start to talk to you about someone else in a gossiping manner (remember that this is how gossips always give themselves away, they talk about others to you as well), you respond by saying something like, 'Oh I really like Carol' then walk off to do something else. This stops them receiving what they were gaining from the gossip – an **interaction/attention.**

The next step is to provide them with as much **interaction/attention** as you can every time they talk about something **more appropriate**. Keep them fully engaged for this kind of conversation. And if the gossip starts to creep in, immediately end the conversation and politely and walk away. You will find that they learn very quickly to modify their behaviour when talking to you. Which can only help when it comes to how they talk with others.

The list is endless as to what outcomes you can achieve when using this strategy for modifying someone's behaviours. It does take some practice but I guarantee that if you are able to apply this process to even some of your life, you will see a decrease in conflict and you will also begin to see people differently to how you did before. Instead of applying an initial judgement when you observe behaviour, you will start to think straight away about what they might be communicating through it.

Toolbox takeaways

- Steps to analysing a person's behaviour are:
    - Step 1: What are they trying to communicate through their behaviour?
    - Step 2: What is the function of the behaviour?
    - Step 3: What is happening in the environment?
    - Step 4: What is the trigger?
    - Step 5: Find a replacement behaviour.
- The replacement behaviour MUST meet the same function as the original behaviour, meaning it MUST provide them with the same need being met, just in a more socially appropriate way.
- Any behaviour you are trying to decrease should have a replacement behaviour you are trying to increase.
- Ask yourself, 'What do I want them to do instead?' or 'What do I want to see instead?'
- You can't just remove a behaviour, that is then the **absence** of a behaviour. Replacing it with another behaviour not only teaches the person a more appropriate way to have their needs met but it increases the likelihood of not reverting to the previous behaviour.
- Remember to reinforce the new behaviour until it becomes routine.
- You can now apply Steps 1–5 in the process of understanding and modifying a person's behaviour.

Replacement Behaviours

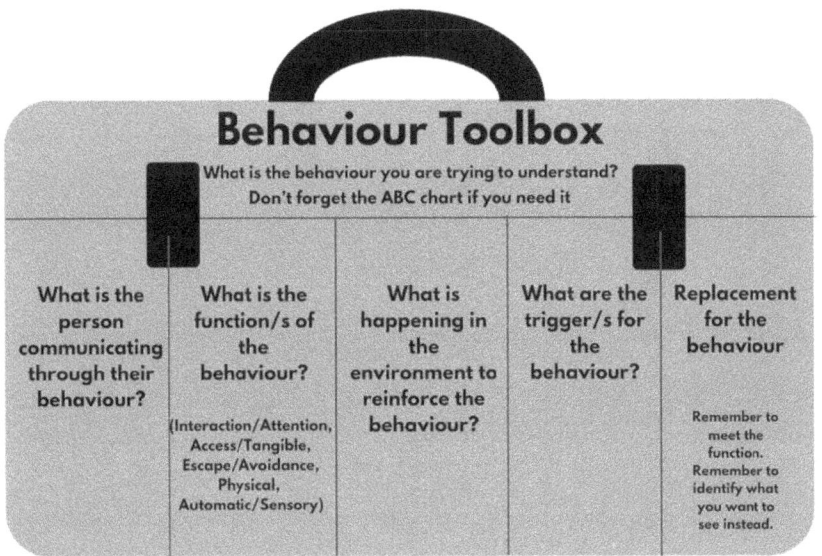

CHAPTER 8

Strategies

◆―――――――◆―――――――◆

At this point in the book, I imagine that you will be beginning to observe people in a different way. Which is what I hope for, that through observing people and their behaviour, you can practise what I have taught you, which will develop and become easier each time you do it. It is not expected that you are suddenly an expert, but that you have reached a point where someone's behaviour makes you stop and think, apply some processes to it and you gain a decent understanding of it. If you are grasping this well, with a bit of practice, you will be applying it and finding replacement behaviours for your everyday interactions. If this is the case, then well done you. If you are struggling with this concept a bit then do not despair, I recommend putting the book down at the end, waiting for a while and then going over it again once you have at least spent some time observing people. Remember that we are all at varying stages of our learning and some of you will pick this up quickly and skip merrily along applying it everywhere, some of you may only ever use the first few chapters and some of you will revisit it in the weeks and months to come. There is no wrong way to use this book.

Regardless of where you sit in the application of this book and the concepts taught in it, there are some strategies you can use along the way, either alongside this book or just in general. That is what this chapter is all about. My top tips for managing behaviour in others.

In behaviour support we provide teams of support workers strategies for supporting their clients. There are two types of strategies that we provide: preventative strategies and response strategies. Preventative strategies are strategies that help to prevent a behaviour from occurring, such as keeping to a person's routine or ensuring that their main triggers are taken care of. In the same way, we can use our own 'preventative strategies' for ensuring our interactions with others are smooth and involve as little conflict as possible. These include communication, modelling, this-then-that, perceived choice and perception of the issue. There is no way for me to give you every single tip and strategy as that would fill a whole book but the five that I have chosen are my absolute top five for managing ANY behaviour. These five will be in every behaviour support plan I send out and if applied well, they will reduce most behaviours significantly.

First, I want to mention the other type of strategies that we use: response strategies. For this, I want to tell you that everything I have taught you up until this point are now your response strategies. Instead of reacting when someone has a behaviour, you can apply the steps 1–5 and you will find that even if you only get to step 1 (what are they communicating through their behaviour) you are going to respond to the person or situation in a very different way than you did before.

Strategies

Communication

My number one tip for every single behaviour and every single dispute, conflict or argument is communication, or effective communication. Effective communication essentially means that you are conveying your message in the way that you meant it and the person is understanding it in the way you meant them to. One of the problems that adds to conflict is that people are scared about communicating their message. They either become too emotionally involved or they worry that the other person will not respond in the way they expect. It therefore leads to us not communicating at all, which in turn leads to further misunderstanding.

Some of the best things you can do to effectively communicate are:

- **Keep very quiet.** One of the biggest challenges I see in the industry I work in, and the world in general, is that people don't know how or when to stay silent, or at least sit quietly when someone else is communicating. If you are trying to work through something such as a conflict or understanding something, then keeping quiet is a good place to start. Which leads me to active listening.
- **Listen – active listening.** Active listening means really listening and hearing what the other person is trying to say. This is different to merely waiting for your chance to speak. You can show that you are actively listening by giving your full attention, not just waiting to speak what is in your head, showing through your body language (this includes not looking at your phone when someone is talking) that you are focused and fully paying attention. If you can master any level of active listening then you are doing well and working toward being an effective communicator.
- **Watch your tone.** Wars have been won and lost in our house based on the tone of voice used by the speaker. Tone really matters and this can be easily demonstrated when considering text messaging. When there is no tone in a

text message it can be very hard to know if the person is being sarcastic, being mean, being sincere, we've all been there. Monitor your tone and notice when it changes.
- **Ask questions**. Most people, but not all, like to talk about themselves or their situation. If you want to be an effective communicator, ask questions. Then keep asking questions to keep the conversation going. Plus, it really helps you to gain plenty of knowledge about a person or a situation if you can ask the right questions.
- **Read the room**. By this I mean read the room, read the person, read the situation. This way you will know when the conversation is coming to an end or if the person is becoming agitated. By reading the situation and watching for change, you can end the conversation when needed or add to the conversation when needed.
- **Control your emotions**. Our emotions get in the way of a lot when we are communicating. If we can control our emotions when communicating we lessen the risk of upsetting someone or becoming even more upset ourselves. My top tip that I use regularly is 'Sleep on it'. If I've received an email that has rattled a few emotions in me, I aim to put it aside until at least the next day so that I can process my annoyance and then hopefully respond without any emotion attached. The same applies to text messages, even though it is expected that you respond quickly. A strategy to use here is to text back immediately and say, 'I'm busy right now so I'll respond to this later. Chat soon'. If it is a face-to-face interaction, then it is perfectly fine to say, 'I need to think about this a bit more, can we talk later when I've had a chance to process it?'.

Modelling

Modelling is your friend when managing behaviours. What I mean by modelling is providing an example of what you want

Strategies

to see. This is true for children and for anyone you are working with. You just apply them in different ways. Modelling works because even though we assume that everyone should know how to behave in every situation, this is often not the case. By modelling, we can provide an example of exactly what we want to see in others. Modelling is probably the strategy you will use more than anything else (aside from effective communication) when managing the behaviour of others. Let me give you a few examples of modelling in action.

Children

When a child uses behaviour and language such as:

'No, it's my turn!' you respond by saying, 'Can I have a turn please?'

'Give me that!' you respond by saying, 'Can I have one please?'

'Nooooo, stop it!' you respond by saying, 'Please stop'

'Fuck off', you respond by saying, 'We don't use that language, instead say, "Please go away"'.

You get the idea. By responding without giving in to emotion, you demonstrate the behaviour you want them to learn.

Adults

With adults it's a bit trickier. But it can still work. Remember in the last chapter, we asked the boss to please bring all requests prior to a suitable time? This is an example of modelling.

Other examples of modelling in adults are:

- If someone speaks poorly or angrily to you, you could simply say, 'Look I understand that you are upset. Could you kindly just ask me instead of shouting, perhaps you could say, "Jeff, I need you to redo that job as it's not up to scratch"'. Obviously, this one is situation specific. You are not going to apply it in a darkened parking lot on a Saturday night with someone who has just run into your car. It's not really the place to say. 'Excuse me sir, how about you learn from my example'. It's probably not going to end well.
- Chairing a meeting, you model the behaviour you want to see in the others who are in attendance.
- In our example on the building site, our person provided a replacement behaviour that was provided in a way that modelled how the interaction should go in the future.

There are thousands of ways to model what you need to happen or the behaviour you expect. A word of caution here, aim to not seem like the expert when you are doing this. I have observed this applied well and I have observed it coming across as righteous. So be mindful of your approach.

Realistic expectations

I wanted to touch on realistic expectations because in my work I often come across really enthusiastic people wanting to action the behaviour suggestions but leap in with both feet and do it all at once. I love their enthusiasm but honestly most behaviour change takes some time and some patience. What I mean by this is that if you are attempting to change your own behaviour of not attending the gym, you are not going to jump right in and start back seven days week. It's likely you've been absent from the gym for a while, so start with going twice a week, stick with that for a while and if it feels okay, add another day and so on.

Strategies

If you are wanting to change your child's routine of emptying the dishwasher, which they keep avoiding, you are not going to just give up if they miss one night. Better to reward what they have completed or set a more realistic goal of them emptying the dishwasher three nights a week and work up to more, rewarding the behaviour you want to see and ignoring the behaviour you don't want to see (within reason).

Realistic expectations set people up for success rather than failure.

This-then-that

One strategy I use over and over is the this-then-that strategy. It's as simple as it sounds and may very well be something you use naturally already. It can help with asking someone to do something without just requesting it or demanding it. I use this with children and adults and it works well when applied the right way.

Instead of saying 'I'd like you to take the garbage out', you could say, 'How about I help you to empty the dishwasher and then you can take out the garbage?'.

Instead of saying, 'I need you to help me develop this spreadsheet', you could say, 'Can you please help me to develop this spreadsheet, then we can go and have lunch together'.

Essentially you are saying – let's do this and then we can do that. It's useful to have a more preferred activity as one of the options but it doesn't have to. It can even work for activities over a longer period, such as 'If you can finish that task by the end of the day then we can go to the movies tomorrow'. Give it a try.

Perceived choice

Ah perceived choice. For some people this strategy is a game changer. Essentially it means that you are providing a person with the perception of having a choice. Not many people in the world like to be told what to do. Most people like to feel that they have choice over themselves and their lives, even children. You can observe this in prisons where almost all choice has been taken away, inmates will still aim to find their individuality by having a choice in how they style their hair or the way they walk and talk. Perceived choice is about the person feeling that they have a choice even when it looks like they don't on the surface.

Let me give you a few examples.

You are trying to complete your morning routine and your child will not get dressed when you ask them to. This happens every morning. You decide to change the way you approach it. Each morning instead of saying, 'Go and put your school clothes on' or 'Can you please get dressed', shift it to saying, 'Do you want to get dressed before or after you have breakfast?' Or, 'Do you want to wear the shorts or the trousers today?'. There are countless ways to reframe a request by highlighting a choice. I use this with adults as well as children and it works well.

Other examples, include:

'Do you want to help me clean up the kitchen before or after your show?'

'Do you want to have your shower before or after dinner?'

'Do you want to get up to the baby tonight or tomorrow night?'

The wonderful thing about this strategy is it actually still tells the person that the task or activity is not negotiable but *when* they do it is negotiable. The only tip I would add is to decide beforehand what your expectation is. For example, if you really need the dishwasher emptied before dinner then it's no point offering anything different. Provide the two options that YOU are most comfortable with.

Perception

When you start to really look at human behaviour (others or your own) you begin to notice how often it becomes a bigger deal than it actually is. Don't get me wrong, there are times when someone's behaviour really is a big deal due to the impact on others. But most of the time we can do well by putting things in perspective against other more important things. What I mean is – it's all about your perception. How one person views a behaviour is going to be very different to how another person views it.

We live in a world where general everyday interactions are sensationalised in the media and in TV shows, which can lead to people modelling this in their own lives. This can increase stress levels, add to conflict, increase anxiety and heighten worries. It is important to try to break a situation down and see it for what it is. What I mean is, how important is this situation that has happened? How much impact does this behaviour have on me or those around me?

We apply importance to events and incidents based a lot on what others around us do and this can skew our perception of how to respond. I find it useful to ask myself some questions when I am in doubt of how to respond to a behaviour, a situation or an incident. My late mother used to say to me, if there was something small that had occurred, 'It is a minor inconvenience in your life', and I find that a very humbling way to look at things so I use it as part of my questioning, alongside others like, 'How big a deal is this?'. Essentially, what I am trying to say is that when you are trying to change or modify a behaviour, 'don't sweat the small stuff'. Have some patience and don't despair if something is taking longer than you thought to change or doesn't change at all and you have to rethink it. At the end of the day behaviour change is a process, not a magic wand. So often I begin working with a family who have the perception that I'm coming in to 'fix' their loved one. While it would be great to have a magic wand, I make sure I explain the process for them so that they understand that it is not a quick fix and effective change can take some time. The same is true for you when using this process. Take some time, allow yourself to make some mistakes along the way and remember that if what you have tried doesn't work, then at least you've ruled something out and you can try something else.

Strategies

Toolbox takeaways

- There are some key tips and strategies that can assist with most behaviours.
    - Communication: Effective communication, such as shutting up, active listening, monitoring your tone, asking questions, reading the room and controlling your emotions.
    - Modelling: Model the behaviour you want to see in others.
    - Realistic expectations: Having realistic expectations will set you up for success rather than failure.
    - This-then-that: Using a this then that strategy can help to lessen the expectation on a person when asked to do something.
    - Perceived choice: Ask someone to do something by using a 'choice question' so the person feels that they have more choice.
    - Perception: How we perceive things helps us navigate change. Behaviour change takes time. Don't sweat the small stuff, if it doesn't work, then try something else.

CHAPTER 9

What About Me?

STUDYING IS ALWAYS GOOD FOR your own self-reflection. As our mind procures greater knowledge, we can apply that new knowledge to our lives with the hope of enhancing them. This was true of my social work degree and it is especially true of behaviour analysis. Turning the view back onto ourselves and truly looking in the behaviour mirror at our past and present behaviour is a life-changing process. However, it can be a hard thing to do. So often, as human beings we point the finger outward, feeling that things are beyond our control due to other people's actions and behaviours. It is certainly a much easier thing to accept, that circumstances are outside our control. The reason for this is that if we feel that circumstances are outside our control or that they are due to someone else's behaviour or actions, then guess what? That means we don't have to DO anything. We can sit back, blame others, blame the universe, blame anyone but ourselves. We don't have to change.

But what if I told you that by reflecting on your own actions, responses and behaviours you would enhance your life and change the way you view others and their behaviours?

Now this is not a trick, I haven't secretly been providing you with all this knowledge only to throw you under the bus and say – actually it's all about you, forget everyone else's behaviour, reflect it all on you.

But some of it is.

While it may not seem like it at times, there is ALWAYS something that you can do to enhance an interaction or a relationship. And behaviour analysis is a great tool to do just that.

I want you to know that analysing your own behaviours is both easier and harder than analysing others. It is harder because of how challenging it can be to admit to ourselves that we have some internal work to do, but it is easier because you have full knowledge of yourself and your internal motivators ready at hand. You know, either deep inside or right on the surface, what you were feeling at the time of a behaviour or what you are feeling now. There is no guessing or making assumptions. We are the experts in our own world and that gives us the antecedent (the trigger), the behaviour and the consequence (the reinforcer) right at our fingertips. We know what we were trying to communicate through our behaviour, we can work out the function of our own behaviour, we know what was happening in the environment and we can easily work out our own triggers.

The exact formula that I have taught you throughout this book can be applied in the same way to yourself as it can be to your family and friend's behaviours. The really great thing about this is that … no-one has to know. Unless you choose to tell them, to admit to things or even apologise for past transgressions. But you don't have to. You can analyse your own behaviour in the privacy of your own head. You can even come up with your own replacement behaviours, try them out and see if they work, then change them if they don't. And no-one ever has to know that you are on this journey of self-reflection.

Let's have a look at the formula and see if we can tweak it to suit a self-reflection on behaviour.

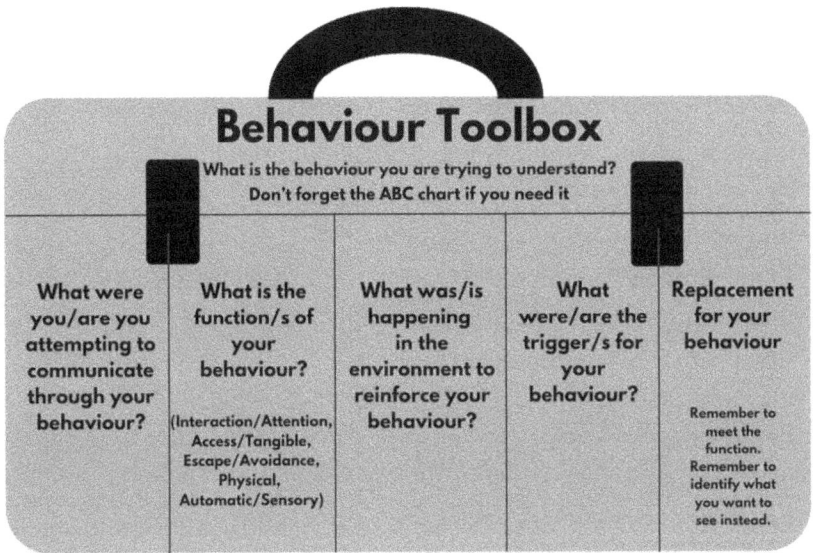

With a few small language tweaks the formula can be applied to you. I think it's worthwhile going through a couple of examples to demonstrate how to apply this to yourself.

Example 1

After reading this chapter you start to think about your own behaviours. You realise that almost every night you end up yelling at your children and your partner. It's usually around the evening mealtime when you are trying to cook food, manage homework with children and prepare bathtimes. You decide to think through the process but end up sitting down, with pencil and paper, to map out what is happening.

Step 1 – What are you trying to communicate to your family when you are yelling?

> **Answer:** Likely you realise that you are trying to communicate that you are finding this really hard, that you are overwhelmed by the tasks and that you could use some help. Obviously, every person is different but we will go with this for now.

Step 2 – What is the function of your behaviour?

Well, I'm going to guess that the function is:

Interaction/attention – the reason is that you are needing a level of attention to your very real needs.

But it is also:

Escape/avoidance – you are most likely very overwhelmed by the situation and you are actually wanting to escape it. Even though you can't feasibly do this.

Step 3 – Let's look at the environment.

You ask yourself the three questions about the environment:

Who is there?

> Your three children are there and your partner. Each are placing demands on you, which is compounding and you are feeling overwhelmed and stressed.

What About Me?

Is there something in the physical environment that is contributing to your behaviour of yelling?

> You realise that the noise of the TV blaring is significantly adding to and impacting on you and your ability to cope.

What in this environment is keeping the behaviour happening or reinforcing the behaviour?

> In this situation the thing that is reinforcing you yelling is that it has become very effective at getting everyone to pause and listen to what you are saying.

Step 4 – What is the trigger?

> Once you write it all down and really think about it, you realise that the actual trigger for your yelling is the volume of noise during that time of the evening.

Step 5 – What is the replacement behaviour?

> In this case, you can easily see that not only do you need a replacement behaviour that provides you with the same function but you notice that if you modify the environment, you will reduce the triggers for the yelling.

If this was me, I'd be looking at the environment first and making it a new rule that the TV remains off until after dinner. One simple environmental factor taken care of, the noise level is reduced and therefore at least one of my triggers is removed or lessened. However, it's likely that this will require some management. Then I'd be thinking, I wonder if I can make additional changes to the environment, which could be something like making bulk meals on the weekend so that there is minimal work on a weeknight. Obviously, these are basic examples and you would need to apply your own solutions.

Once I had looked at reducing the environmental triggers, I would then explore what a replacement behaviour could be for my own behaviour of yelling. There is no one firm answer for this but some things I would explore are:

- Having a conversation with my partner to say, 'I am struggling with managing this time, I need you to help balance the workload' and then work out how this can happen. **(interaction/attention)**
- I could look at taking myself out of the room for 5–10 minutes, taking some deep breaths **(escape/avoidance)**
- I could have my earbuds in and have calming music playing **(escape/avoidance)**.

The list goes on and only you will know the best replacement for your own behaviour. The only word of caution here is to remember to reinforce the new behaviour. For example, the new way of dealing with things has to be reinforced or it won't be sustainable. Remember the reinforcement just means that it is still meeting your need.

Let's try another one.

Example 2

Let's say that you regularly end up drinking way too much alcohol, late into the night with one friend in particular, which is upsetting your partner, your routine and your health as you are feeling pretty awful the next day and you are finding that it is increasing your anxiety in general. You decide to do something about it and because you have read this book and you know how to analyse the behaviour you give it a go.

Step 1 – What are you communicating through your behaviour?

What About Me?

Answer: Hmm, this is a tricky one. I'd be thinking that I was communicating my need for a social interaction with my friend and possibly a break from my day-to-day life. (Hint: the function is almost revealing itself in this one.)

Step 2 – What is the function of this behaviour?

I'm hoping by now that you were able to identify at least one of the functions of this behaviour. I think there's more than one.

- **Interaction/attention**: You are needing an interaction with someone other than your family.
- **Access/tangible**: You are attempting to gain access to time with your friend.
- **Escape/avoidance**: Possibly you are needing an escape from your everyday routine.

Step 3 – Let's look at the environment. Ask yourself the three questions:

Who is there?

> Your friend has called in to see you on a regular day of the week.

Is there something in the physical environment that is contributing to your behaviour?

> Possibly easy access and being comfortable in the space.

What in this environment is keeping the behaviour happening or reinforcing the behaviour?

> You realise that the reinforcer is internally driven as it provides you with the elated feelings of happiness when being intoxicated.

Step 4 – What is the trigger?

You realise that the trigger is now the day of the week as your friend has been coming in to see you on the same day each week for months. You also realise that the trigger is now seeing this one particular friend. But don't despair, it doesn't mean you have to ditch this friend to change the behaviour. Let's look at the final step to find out how to replace this behaviour and still meet the function.

Step 5 – What is the replacement behaviour?

I think the replacement behaviour could be something similar to the following, depending on your interests:

- You stick with the day of the week to meet up with your friend but you change the location
- You agree to a mutual activity, let's say playing a round of golf (or whatever activity you enjoy)
- You lock it in place and make sure that you both agree to stick with it for the next six weeks.

This example demonstrates how one simple change can immediately meet all the functions of the behaviour. It provides the interaction you were needing with your friend, it provides access to a specific person, your friend, and it most likely provides you the escape you were needing as well. Simple right?

Assessing our own behaviours is a marvellous way to practise the process of following the five steps to managing behaviours. You can practise and practise until you are feeling confident enough to apply this to the outside world. If you get it wrong or not quite right, it doesn't matter, you can start over. Try and then try again.

Many years ago, when most of my children were in full-time school, I chose to work four days a week instead of five, for a couple of reasons. One was that it wasn't financially viable to work the fifth day due to tax brackets and it was to give me one day a week to get all the extra things completed, such as paying bills, grocery shopping, washing the car, getting through a few loads of washing, that type of thing. The idea being that if I had this day to catch up on things then the rest of the week would be much easier.

What ended up happening is that I would inevitably make an excuse to head out early on my day off to take care of things and would often wander around a shop browsing, going to a café for a nice quiet lunch without children, then come home, bake some sweet treats for the children and inadvertently 'waste the day'.

I have thought about this one quite a bit and I believe if I had the knowledge I have now in analysing my own behaviour I could have easily observed that I was seriously needing an escape. The escape function would be clear and I would then apply a replacement behaviour to the situation and hopefully achieve more from my one day off a week! I imagine if I were to go back in time and apply this process to my behaviour, I would try actually giving myself the real break I needed by having a massage or a brunch in the morning to meet the escape function and then proceeding through the day with all the other things I needed to do. It wasn't all bad. I would often quickly and frantically do all the things I needed to in the last hour of my day off, but it could have been much smoother and less stressful if I'd known a different way to look at it.

One of the main reasons for turning the analyses inward and assessing our own behaviours, is that it changes how we view others. Once you are aware of your own drivers behind your behaviour it becomes significantly harder to judge other people for theirs. It becomes almost a superpower that you can apply to all areas of your life. The beauty of this process is that it actually doesn't matter who you are, where you live, what you earn, what you drive, what you look like – this process can be applied to every person and almost every behaviour.

By thoroughly and extensively examining yourself and your behaviours, both past and present, you gain a much deeper insight into your communication style, your internal drivers, your motivations, your bad habits (and your good ones). I guarantee that if you continue to apply this to your own life, you will become much more skilled in applying it without writing it down or even going through the process step by step. You will reach a point when you can do it all in your head, which makes it much easier to apply in day-to-day interactions. You will also notice that your actual responses become much more considered and that you very rarely 'react' to a situation. All of these advantages are great for other people interacting with you but more than anything by having this level of understanding you will feel more peaceful in your approach to others as you have knowledge that mitigates almost any situation. I truly hope you get to see this in your life through this process.

Toolbox takeaways

- Steps to analysing your own behaviour are:
    - Step 1: What was I/am I trying to communicate through my behaviour?
    - Step 2: What is the function of my behaviour?
    - Step 3: What is happening in the environment?
    - Step 4: What is the trigger?
    - Step 5: Find a replacement behaviour.
- Looking inward at your own behaviour can be challenging.
- You can apply the process of the five steps to your own behaviour in exactly the same way as applying it to another persons' behaviour.
- Analysing your own behaviour is harder in some ways due to it being hard to admit that we have some internal work to do.
- Analysing your own behaviour is easier in some ways as all the information is in your own head.
- Working out the reasons behind your own behaviours is life-changing and it will modify how you view others and their behaviour.
- Analysing your own behaviour is the best practice for analysing others.
- Remember – no-one has to know that you are analysing your own behaviour or making changes to it.
- You can now apply Steps 1–5 in the process of understanding and modifying YOUR OWN behaviour.

CHAPTER 10

Neurodiversity

YOU MAY BE WONDERING WHY I have chosen to include a chapter on neurodiversity in this book. There are a number of reasons, including creating an ongoing awareness within our world. However, one of the most important reasons for including this chapter is that often people who are neurodivergent are the most misunderstood, which equates to increased behaviours. This in turn can lead to fear or uncertainty around how to interact with someone who is neurodivergent. I have included this chapter to try to answer some common questions about this and to increase awareness of our deeply neurodiverse society. This is important as more and more of our workplaces are becoming inclusive and neurodivergent people are able to be employed in jobs that would not have been previously available to them. It is highly likely that you now have a coworker who is neurodivergent, which is exciting but may require some modifications to ensure they feel accepted or at least included.

What actually is neurodiversity and how does this differ from neurodivergent? Even though it can seem that the two terms are used interchangeably, the term neurodiverse refers to a group of people who are neurodivergent and so the individual would be referred to as being neurodivergent. For example, a school might have a diverse student body due to having a number of neurodivergent students who attend.

Neurodivergent = An individual whose brain functioning is divergent from the majority of society

Neurotypical = An individual whose brain functioning is typical of the majority of society

Neurodiverse = Refers to a group of people, with potentially different forms of neurodivergence

An individual who is neurodivergent would typically have a diagnosis that includes but is not exclusive to: Autism spectrum, ADHD (attention deficit hyperactivity disorder), dyslexia, dyscalculia and dyspraxia. However, as this is a rapidly changing space, it is important to be aware that this may look vastly different in the future with additional diagnosis being included under the umbrella of neurodivergent.

People with a disability of any category or diagnosis, want to be treated with dignity and to have access to every opportunity that they would have access to if they did not have a disability, even if it means an accommodation is made. The same is true of anyone who is neurodivergent. However, we often hear of people complaining about adjustments that need to be made to accommodate someone's disability. I won't give examples of some of the comments I have heard as I don't want to give them room in this book but they are usually cited by people who have not experienced any sort of disadvantage that was out of their control. The important thing is that when we are accommodating someone who is neurodivergent or has a disability, it is essential that we listen to their individual needs and not just place a blanket adjustment that we think should 'fix everything'. The way to find this out is to ask the person, if appropriate, if there's anything they require that you can assist with. The person will either say no or they will give you an outline of any accommodations that would assist them. Asking is important as many well-meaning people have made assumptions and just leap in to 'help' without checking with the person first. So please just ask, don't assume.

I am going to outline some additional tips for working with anyone with a disability or someone who is neurodivergent so that you can use this to assist in the world and pass these tips on to others as needed.

Processing variations

My first tip is that people who are neurodivergent sometimes process information in different ways to neurotypical people. What I mean by this is that they may have additional skills or skill deficits that can be vastly different to a neurotypical person. What is important about this is that more and more we are recognising that the variants in processing are suited to a range of jobs that enhance the outcome. Examples of variations in processing can include: hyper focusing, where a person has a very intense focus on one task or topic in particular to the exclusion of other things; recognising patterns, where a person may have a strength in being able to see or recognise patterns where others cannot; non-linear thinking which can often lead to creative problem solving; processing speed differences, where someone is able to either process information extremely rapidly or much more slowly (be mindful of this when talking with someone who is neurodivergent as you may need to adjust your own speed to accommodate); processing social differences, such as differences in understanding social cues and emotions, which can impact communication; and processing requiring multi-sensory processes such as visual or tactile methods alongside verbal communication.

Communication

People who are neurodivergent can struggle with very abstract information or instructions. What I mean by abstract is that it is not direct and clear. For example, if I were to say to someone, 'Can you please make sure that you tidy up all your files?' this might mean something completely different to different people. One person might see this as meaning to check all aspects of the files and another might think it means to fix any problems you find. The same is true if you say to a child, 'I need you to be good'. This is a very abstract term as what good means to one person can be completely different to another person's perception. Much better to say exactly what your expectation is so that the meaning is clear to both the communicator and the person hearing it. Instead of 'Tidy up your files', you could say, 'Can you please check each file to ensure that all the documents are uploaded and there are no outstanding actions?'. The same is true for the example of 'good' behaviour. Better to say exactly what the expectation is. For example, 'I need you to please sit still during the show and no talking until the end'. This is a much clearer expectation than just 'be good' and it works for everyone, both neurotypical and neurodivergent.

Routines

One of the most challenging things in life for people who are neurodivergent are routines. At the same time routines can really assist someone who is neurodivergent to accomplish goals or targets. And so, I suggest a *flexible routine*. This is something I used throughout my years of parenting five children. Having a flexible routine provided enough routine to keep things moving and not falling apart but with flexibility so that if a spanner was thrown into the works, then we could still function as a family without it becoming something resembling a nuclear disaster. Some of the reasons routines can be challenging for neurodivergent folk is that there are often unexpected factors within the environment that they have to navigate in creative ways as well as factors from within them that impact on being able to navigate the environment. For example, routines often involve predictable environments but this can be impacted by unexpected sensory stimuli such as loud noises or bright lights. Routines also have a component of predictability and repetition to them, which can be challenging for someone who struggles if something changes suddenly, as they may not be able to easily rethink the processes. Other neurodivergent people may struggle with the social interaction of a routine or sustaining the attention of a routine or even the demands that having a routine places on them. A flexible routine provides the best of both worlds.

Impulse control

Being able to control impulses can be a significant challenge for someone who is neurodivergent. It can be a challenge for people who are neurotypical too but it is more common in the neurodivergent world. One of the best strategies that helps with impulse control has already been mentioned in this book. Triggers. Identifying the triggers really helps to manage impulsivity. Once you have analysed this behaviour or the associated behaviours (remember it is easier to analyse individual behaviours than a whole general pattern), you are able to predict when you might have this happen again or be able to recognise it when it is happening. The second tip is to stop and reflect on what you are doing. This can be as simple as stopping, taking three (or 10) deep breaths and if possible, remove yourself from the environment. By taking this small step it can interrupt the process of being impulsive and give you time to reassess choices. The third tip for managing impulse control is to learn to delay gratification. This means to teach yourself or others to wait a specified and agreed upon amount of time before having what it is that you want. The idea being that you slowly increase the delay over time. Using any or all of these strategies can assist in managing impulse control over time.

Executive functioning

Ah this old chestnut. So often talked about but what are the challenges and what can we do to help? Executive functioning is an area that impacts those who are neurodivergent significantly. It encompasses a range of skills, including: planning and prioritising, organisation, working memory, time management, attention, flexibility, impulse control, emotional control, task initiation and self-monitoring. It is important to know that not every neurodivergent person is impacted by every executive functioning area. For some they may only struggle with one or two areas, for others it can be almost all of them. That is why we cannot place all neurodiverse people into one category or apply one set of rules. Instead, we can try a range of strategies to address each area until we find what works best. For example, a person who struggles with time management could set timers, break tasks up into timed intervals and schedule regular breaks for themselves. Someone who struggles with planning and prioritising might try using a calendar and a diary and a planner, until they find the combination that works for them. They might download an app to their phone with set tasks and reminders. There are so many options out there to assist with supporting executive functioning that you only need to search online and you will be inundated with possibilities. Which leads me to my next heading.

Overwhelm

We have all been overwhelmed by tasks or pressures in our lives, but for neurodivergent people, it can be much worse. This can be due to having a lower threshold, processing difficulties, sensory sensitivities or a range of other challenges. My tips for supporting overwhelm include: removing any demands that are not important, sleeping on it, tackling one task at a time (and if that is too much then tackling one aspect of a task at a time), asking for help, taking a break, completing tasks from hardest to easiest OR completing tasks from easiest to hardest, whatever works for your brain or the brain of the person you are supporting. The main thing to remember is that what works for one person may not work for another, it's therefore important to try different things until you find what works for you. You may even find that what worked for you in one circumstance might not work for you in another. Different settings require different strategies, which is important to remember when supporting someone who is neurodivergent.

Demands

The final area I want to touch on in this chapter is demands. There is a growing awareness of demands, what they are and how to navigate them in our society. Some of this awareness stems from variations in the presentation of some autism diagnosis. One of these is pathological demand avoidance profile (PDA), which is a profile of autism with particular traits that impact on functioning. The reason I want to add this is that throughout my work in behaviour support I have found that even without a specific diagnosis, many people who are neurodivergent either struggle with or are impacted by what are known as 'demands'. Demands can be just about anything but for the purpose of this description I am going to focus on the most common ones that are either obvious or unseen. Demands can include (but are not exclusive to): plans, routines, decisions, transitions, expectations (internal or external), time, deadlines, praise, internal body demands, questions and many more. Demands can contribute to overwhelm and other challenges. However, a word of caution, just because you struggle with demand does not mean you have a PDA profile or have autism. I am just pointing it out here so that you can have an awareness of how to manage this in someone who is demand-sensitive.

If you or someone you support have challenges with demands, the following strategies are my best tips. Remember perceived choice that I mentioned in Chapter 8? It is my number one tip for reducing demands. By framing up the task as a choice you are reducing the demand on the person. Alongside this is using indirect language, for example, 'It would be useful if you made your bed'. Creating a low arousal or low stress environment is a great way to reduce demands as it reduces the stress around the person. And finally, have a plethora of backup plans so that if things fall apart, you have a backup or a contingency plan.

Final thoughts on neurodiversity

You are probably wondering if there is anything specific you need to know about analysing behaviour in someone who has a disability or is neurodivergent and the answer is, not really. The beautiful thing about this process is it remains the same whether a person is neurodivergent, neurotypical, has a disability or disorder. It is applied in exactly the same manner. There are some obvious challenges when it comes to obtaining information, if someone is non-verbal or has significant challenges to their receptive and expressive language, but it still works. Just ensure that you utilise your skills and knowledge of working with neurodiversity to ensure that you are working in a respectful way. The rest of the process is exactly the same, whether you are supporting someone in your workplace or your family.

As our society continues to evolve and change, opportunities for people who have additional challenges in their lives, such as a disability or neurodiversity, continue to grow. As a person who grew up in a time where people with disability were often ostracised, ridiculed and taunted, it warms my heart to now see the beautiful way that people are supported. In my role as a behaviour support practitioner, I hear the best and the worst of people who are actively working in the disability sector. Luckily, I mostly hear good and anything that is not great is reported and followed up. Certainly, there are things that are missed, and these are the ones we see in the media. But these are a minority and there is more good happening, by far, than bad. Well, from what I see anyway.

The point I am trying to make is, as our society continues to evolve to be more inclusive, it becomes more and more important to understand diversity and know how to support inclusion. So, if this chapter provides even a small step towards that then I am happy.

Toolbox takeaways

- People who are neurodivergent are the most misunderstood, which equates to increased behaviours.
- The term neurodiverse refers to a group of people who are neurodivergent and so the individual would be referred to as being neurodivergent.
- Key terms are:
  - **Neurodivergent** = An individual whose brain functioning is divergent from the majority of society
  - **Neurotypical** = An individual whose brain functioning is typical of the majority of society
  - **Neurodiverse** = Refers to a group of people, with potentially different forms of neurodivergence.
- Neurodivergent diagnosis includes but is not exclusive to: autism spectrum, ADHD (attention deficit hyperactivity disorder), dyslexia, dyscalculia and dyspraxia.
- Neurodiverse groups of people have multiple challenges they face that are in addition to challenges faced by neurotypical people. Some things that can be adjusted to support this include:
  - **Processing variations**
  - **Communication**
  - **Routines**
  - **Impulse control**
  - **Executive functioning**
  - **Demands**.
- Neurodiversity is an evolving and varied space that will become a spectrum of variation for every person, so that there is no expected 'normal' for a person's skills and challenges to measure against.

CHAPTER 11

Summary and Pulling it all Together

I HOPE THAT BY REACHING this chapter that you have stuck with the book and I have been able to keep your interest in what can, honestly, be quite a dry topic. It was always going to be the greatest challenge as a writer, for it to not bore you into a deep slumber halfway through a chapter. Additionally, the challenge was to bring a huge extensive topic of behaviour analysis into a user-friendly process for everyday people in five easy steps. I hope I have achieved that and that you are ready and able to put the process into practice.

As a final discussion I want to go over each stage of the behaviour process and look again at the full toolbox of behaviour tools, as well as recounting the chapter takeaways in one place. I then want to discuss ways that you can use this in your own life. Which I think extends to just about anything.

As a recap, in Chapter 1, we dove into the theorists, essentially the main contributors to behaviour analysis and what they had each brought to the discipline of behaviour. While there have been many other contributors to this area, the four that I mentioned, Ivan Pavlov, Edward Thorndike, John Watson and B.F. Skinner, had significant contributions and remain the forefathers of this school of thought. We also touched on one of the current uses of behaviour analysis in Australia, which is behaviour support through the National Disability Insurance Scheme (NDIS), including a very important point, that we strive to not use purely applied behaviour analysis (ABA) processes, opting instead for more person-centred approaches.

In Chapter 2, we discussed and explored that all behaviour is actually communication. We unpacked some examples to highlight that this is true. Additionally, we explored the behaviour iceberg, which demonstrated that while behaviour sits above the water in the iceberg analogy, everything that sits below the water is key in understanding a behaviour. Toward the end of the chapter, we were reminded that communication through behaviour can be conscious or unconscious as well as being communicated in both positive or negative ways.

In Chapters 3–7, I then took you through the main features of the understanding behaviour process, adding a new tool to your toolbox each step along the way. This included the function of behaviour, assessing the environment, considering triggers and finally looking at ways to find a replacement behaviour for others or yourself, culminating in our full toolbox.

Summary and Pulling it all Together

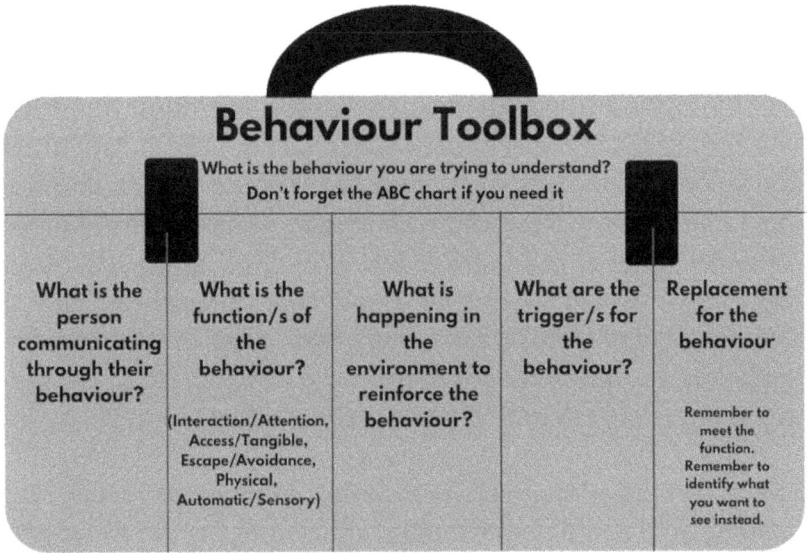

For Chapters 8–10, I presented you with some strategies, some modelling, the all-important chapter called 'What About Me?' where we shone the light on ourselves and how to modify our own behaviour, finishing with some tips and an overview of neurodiversity.

So, what now?

It is essentially up you how you use this information moving forward. You can tuck this book away and keep the knowledge sitting neatly in your mind, awaiting the perfect opportunity to apply it to an unsuspecting person. Or you can keep it fresh in your mind, going over it in detail and checking through the process each and every time you come across a behaviour you don't understand. Some people will spend a great deal of time on themselves first and foremost before branching out to understanding other people's behaviour. However you use it, the knowledge serves a purpose and can assist you to have an experience with others that is hopefully smoother and with less conflict.

Perhaps you are a teacher and you are able to use this knowledge to enhance your understanding of the neurodivergent child in your classroom. Or maybe you are a tradie who can use this process to not only get along with your coworkers but create smoother relationships with customers. It may be that you work in an office in a large team and you are now able to understand the office dynamics better or know how to work with the gossip on the team. Right across to having a toddler, a small child or a teenager, or you simply have a partner or friends who you can now understand in deeper ways. Whatever it is, these have been my hopes for you as the reader as I shared this information with you.

I have created throughout the book some easy to review, key features, which include the toolbox visuals, the chapter takeaways at the end of each chapter and a plethora of examples to assist in your understanding of behaviour. To make this even easier I will now lay out each chapter's takeaways so that you don't have to go flicking through the book to find them. It's a nice easy way to recap when you need.

Takeaways and key points

Chapter 1 takeaways

- This chapter's background information provides you with the empty toolbox that is the foundation of where behaviour analysis and my role in it has come from.
- Curiosity about behaviour is where it all begins.
- The foundational ideas by psychological theorists are still relevant to today's understanding of behaviour.
- Classical conditioning, operant conditioning and law and effect are key terms in psychological behaviour analysis.
- Behaviours of concern is a term used by the National Disability Insurance Scheme (NDIS) to describe any behaviours that are deemed 'undesirable behaviours'.

- Applied behaviour analysis (ABA), which forms a lot of the foundations of understanding behaviour, is not as popular as it once was in providing alternatives to behaviour.

Chapter 2 takeaways

- All behaviour is communicating something.
- Behaviour can communicate in positive or negative ways.
- Behaviour communication is like an iceberg, the behaviour can be seen above the water and what is being communicated sits below the water.
- Just because a behaviour is illegal or morally abhorrent, doesn't mean we can't work out what is being communicated.
- Communication through behaviour can be conscious or unconscious.
- People under the influence of substances will communicate with their behaviour more than those who are sober.

Chapter 3 takeaways

- Steps to analysing a person's behaviour are:
    - Step 1: What are they trying to communicate through their behaviour?
    - Step 2: What is the function of the behaviour?
- There are five functions of behaviour – interaction/attention, access/tangible, escape/avoidance, automatic/sensory and physical.
- Understanding the function enables us to work out the WHY of the behaviour.
- Knowing the function can help us know how to respond to a behaviour to either eliminate it or reduce it.
- Understanding the behaviour and knowing the function doesn't mean we have to agree with it or the person having the behaviour.

Chapter 4 takeaways

- Steps to analysing a person's behaviour are:
    - Step 1: What are they trying to communicate through their behaviour?
    - Step 2: What is the function of the behaviour?
- There are five functions of behaviour – interaction/attention, access/tangible, escape/avoidance, automatic/sensory and physical.
- Some behaviours have more than one function.
- If you are unclear on what the function might be, use the ABC chart to help.

Chapter 5 takeaways

- Steps to analysing a person's behaviour are:
    - Step 1: What are they trying to communicate through their behaviour?
    - Step 2: What is the function of the behaviour?
    - Step 3: What is happening in the environment?
- There are five functions of behaviour – interaction/attention, access/tangible, escape/avoidance, automatic/sensory and physical.
- Understanding the environment can help to understand the behaviour.
- Ask yourself three key questions about the environment:
    - Who is there?
    - Is there something in the physical environment contributing to the behaviour?
    - What in this environment is keeping the behaviour happening or reinforcing the behaviour?
- Look for the reinforcers of the behaviour.
- Remember: **A behaviour cannot exist or remain without something reinforcing it.**

Summary and Pulling it all Together

Chapter 6 takeaways

- Steps to analysing a person's behaviour are:
    - Step 1: What are they trying to communicate through their behaviour?
    - Step 2: What is the function of the behaviour?
    - Step 3: What is happening in the environment?
    - Step 4: What is the trigger?
- A trigger is the antecedent or the thing that happens before the behaviour happens.
- By knowing the trigger, you can predict when a behaviour will be more likely to happen again.
- You can now apply Steps 1–4 in the process of understanding a person's behaviour.
- **There is ALWAYS a trigger even if it is not obvious, you just have to work it out.**

Chapter 7 takeaways

- Steps to analysing a person's behaviour are:
    - Step 1: What are they trying to communicate through their behaviour?
    - Step 2: What is the function of the behaviour?
    - Step 3: What is happening in the environment?
    - Step 4: What is the trigger?
    - Step 5: Find a replacement behaviour.
- The replacement behaviour MUST meet the same function as the original behaviour, meaning it MUST provide them with the same need being met, just in a more socially appropriate way.
- **Any behaviour you are trying to decrease should have a replacement behaviour you are trying to increase.**
- Ask yourself, 'What do I want them to do instead?' or 'What do I want to see instead?'.

- You can't just remove a behaviour, that is then the **absence** of a behaviour. Replacing it with another behaviour not only teaches the person a more appropriate way to have their needs met but it increases the likelihood of not reverting to the previous behaviour.
- Remember to reinforce the new behaviour until it becomes routine.
- You can now apply Steps 1–5 in the process of understanding and modifying a person's behaviour.

Chapter 8 takeaways

- There are some key tips and strategies that can assist with most behaviours.
- Communication: Effective communication, such as shutting up, active listening, monitoring your tone, asking questions, reading the room and controlling your emotions.
- Modelling: Model the behaviour you want to see in others.
- Realistic expectations: Having realistic expectations will set you up for success rather than failure.
- This-then-that: Using a this then that strategy can help to lessen the expectation on a person when asked to do something.
- Perceived choice: Ask someone to do something by using a 'choice question' so the person feels that they have more choice.
- Perception: How we perceive things helps us navigate change. Behaviour change takes time; don't sweat the small stuff. If it doesn't work, then try something else.

Summary and Pulling it all Together

Chapter 9 takeaways

- Steps to analysing your own behaviour are:
    - Step 1: What was I/am I trying to communicate through my behaviour?
    - Step 2: What is the function of my behaviour?
    - Step 3: What is happening in the environment?
    - Step 4: What is the trigger?
    - Step 5: Find a replacement behaviour.
- Looking inward at your own behaviour can be challenging.
- You can apply the process of the five steps to your own behaviour in exactly the same way as applying it to another person's behaviour.
- Analysing your own behaviour is harder in some ways due to it being hard to admit that we have some internal work to do.
- Analysing your own behaviour is easier in some ways as all the information is in your own head.
- Working out the reasons behind your own behaviours is life-changing and it will modify how you view others and their behaviour.
- Analysing your own behaviour is the best practice for analysing others.
- Remember – no-one has to know that you are analysing your own behaviour or making changes to it.
- You can now apply Steps 1–5 in the process of understanding and modifying YOUR OWN behaviour.

Chapter 10 takeaways

- People who are neurodivergent are the most misunderstood, which equates to increased behaviours.
- The term neurodiverse refers to a group of people who are neurodivergent and so the individual would be referred to as being neurodivergent.

- Key terms are:
    - **Neurodivergent** = An individual whose brain functioning is divergent from the majority of society
    - **Neurotypical** = An individual whose brain functioning is typical of the majority of society
    - **Neurodiverse** = Refers to a group of people, with potentially different forms of neurodivergence.
- Neurodivergent diagnosis includes but is not exclusive to: autism spectrum, ADHD (attention deficit hyperactivity disorder), dyslexia, dyscalculia and dyspraxia.
- Neurodiverse groups of people have multiple challenges they face that are in addition to challenges faced by neurotypical people. Some things that can be adjusted to support this include:
    - **Processing variations**
    - **Communication**
    - **Routines**
    - **Impulse control**
    - **Executive functioning**
    - **Demands**.
- Neurodiversity is an evolving and varied space that will become a spectrum of variation for every person, so that there is no expected 'normal' for a person's skills and challenges to be measured against.

The final feature I have added is an appendix with all of the visuals and diagrams I have used throughout the book. I have extended some of them to make them a printable version that you can add your own information when analysing someone's behaviour. In the appendix you will find user-friendly versions of the following:

- The toolbox (in table format) of behaviour tools so you can map out the five steps for any behaviour as many times as you need
- An ABC chart that incorporates the 'T' for Triggers and the 'R' for reinforcer

Summary and Pulling it all Together

Finally, I encourage you to take your time to work through the process of understanding other people's behaviour. I promise you that the more you practise this process, the easier it becomes and you will eventually be able to do it all in your head without any prompts or tables to help.

More than anything, I strongly encourage you to take a deep look at your own behaviour. Once you push past the uncomfortable feeling of looking inward and facing your own truths head on, it can be quite addictive and you feel incredibly empowered and more in control of yourself. And what more could a person want than that?

Appendix

The Naughty Behaviourist

Behaviour Toolbox

What is the behaviour you are trying to understand?

Don't forget the ABC chart if you need it

Replacement for the behaviour *Remember to meet the function. Remember to identify what you want to see instead*				
What are the Trigger/s for the behaviour?				
What is happening in the environment to reinforce the behaviour?				
What is the function/s of the behaviour? (interaction/attention, access/tangible, escape/avoidance, physical, automatic/sensory)				
What is the person communicating through their behaviour?				

This behaviour toolbox is available at www.marandagraham.com as a pdf for downloading at you convenience.

Appendix

Antecedent/Trigger	Behaviour	Consequence/Reinforcer

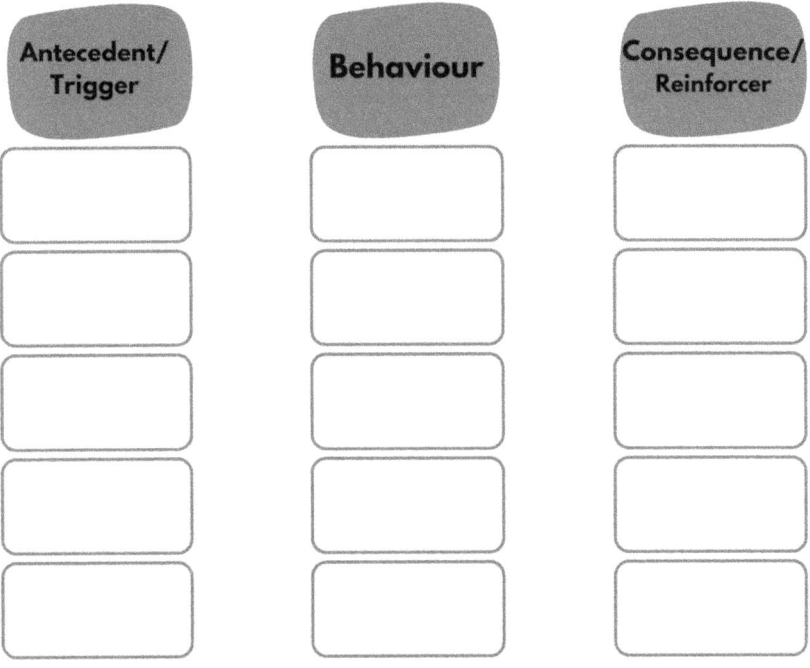

143

About the Author

MARANDA IS A UNIVERSITY QUALIFIED social worker who worked in the homelessness and disability sectors for over a decade, before branching into behaviour support in 2020. Today, in her role as behaviour support practitioner, Maranda works with highly vulnerable individuals and those who support them, providing them with a framework for managing behaviours.

Over the years, Maranda has developed a keen interest in the behaviour of others, and through her work assists her clients, both adult and children, neurotypical and neurodiverse, to find alternatives to challenging behaviours, further enhancing their quality of life.

A keen writer, it has always been Maranda's dream to move into full-time writing, authoring both fiction and non-fiction books. *The Naughty Behaviourist* is her first book.

Maranda was born in Australia and travelled the world throughout her childhood, finally settling in rural Tasmania, where she married and has raised five children. She and her husband enjoy attending live music concerts, comedy shows, walking and spending time as a family.

Maranda is currently working on her first fiction novel, *Trespasses*, which is due for release in Mid 2025.

Notes

The Naughty Behaviourist

Notes

The Naughty Behaviourist

Notes

www.ingramcontent.com/pod-product-compliance
Lightning Source LLC
Chambersburg PA
CBHW041307110526
44590CB00028B/4281